MASS-OBSERVATION ARCHIVE

PAPERS FROM THE MASS-OBSERVATION ARCHIVE AT THE UNIVERSITY OF SUSSEX

Part 7: Topic Collections - Air-Raids, Morale and the Blitz
Part 8: Topic Collections - Conscription, Pacifism and War Service

A Listing and Guide to the microfilm collection

MASS-OBSERVATION ARCHIVE

PAPERS FROM THE MASS-OBSERVATION ARCHIVE AT THE UNIVERSITY OF SUSSEX

Part 7: Topic Collections - Air-Raids, Morale and the Blitz

AIR-RAIDS; PROPAGANDA AND MORALE; LONDON SURVEY, 1940

Part 8: Topic Collections - Conscription, Pacifism and War Service

CONSCIENTIOUS OBJECTION AND PACIFISM; FORCES (MEN); GAS MASKS; DOGS IN WARTIME

A Listing and Guide to the microfilm collection

Adam Matthew Publications

ADAM MATTHEW PUBLICATIONS LTD
Pelham House, London Road
Marlborough
Wiltshire SN8 2AA

MASS-OBSERVATION ARCHIVE
PAPERS FROM THE MASS-OBSERVATION ARCHIVE AT THE UNIVERSITY OF SUSSEX
Part 7: Topic Collections - Air-Raids, Morale and the Blitz
Part 8: Topic Collections - Conscription, Pacifism and War Service
A Listing and Guide to the microfilm collection

First published in 2006 by Adam Matthew Publications Ltd

Printed by Antony Rowe Ltd, Chippenham, Wiltshire
on neutral-sized paper with a ph value of 7.0

British Library Cataloguing in Publication Data

Mass-Observation Archive : papers from the Mass-Observation Archive at the University of Sussex : a listing and guide to parts 7 & 8 of the microfilm collection
1.Mass-Observation. Archive 2.Documents on microfilm - Catalogs
3.Great Britain - Social conditions - 20th century - Archives - Microform catalogs
016.3'06'0941

ISBN 1 85711 264 4

CONTENTS

Dog fights (TC 23, Box 4)

PUBLISHER'S NOTE

"Mass-Observation can be described as a project designed to involve the mass of "ordinary people" in a sociological research process - an "anthropology at home" - as a way of harnessing and explicating "public opinion" as well as, relatedly, helping close the gap between the decision-making of political leaders and the convictions and wishes of ordinary people. Its history is entwined in complex and fascinating ways with the history of the disciplines of anthropology, economics and particularly with sociology".

Liz Stanley, Professor of Sociology , Manchester University
writing in *The Archaeology of a 1930's Mass-Observation Project*

The Mass-Observation Archive is an indispensable source for all those interested in Britain in the 1930's, the home front during World War II and the post-war history of Britain. Researchers are able to discover the views and feelings of ordinary people, through descriptive accounts of their experience and transcribed interviews, on a fascinating range of subjects such as housing, sport, fascism, communism, work, social conditions, religion, cinema, holidays, the onset of war, evacuation, rationing, the Blitz, public morale, post-war hopes, the welfare state, household budgeting, entertainment, shopping, education, the police, public health, trade unions, politics, strikes, transport, royalty, jazz, family planning, industry and drinking habits.

Mass-Observation was the result of three researchers engaged in social investigation who came together by coincidence. Charles Madge, poet and journalist, and Humphrey Jennings, a documentary film maker, envisaged a London-based project in which a national panel of volunteers would reply to regular questionnaires on a variety of subjects. Tom Harrisson, an anthropologist who had worked in Borneo and the New Hebrides, had ideas for an anthropological survey of the British starting with a study of Bolton.

They met, by chance, on the pages of the *New Statesmen* in January 1937 where a poem by Harrisson on the culinary habits of South Sea cannibals appeared on the same page as a letter by Madge announcing that a group of poets, painters and documentary film-makers in Blackheath, London, intended to start an *"anthropology of ourselves"* to explore the role of myth and superstition in national life and the gulf between public opinion and what was often described as public opinion by the Government and in the Press. They corresponded and on 30 January 1937 a further letter appeared in the *New Statesman* signed by Madge, Jennings and Harrisson formally announcing the creation of Mass-Observation.

In February 1937 Madge and Harrisson issued *Mass-Observation*, setting out the aims of the group and describing observers as *"meteorological stations from whose reports a weather map of popular feeling can be compiled."* The emphasis was on a true, detached, scientific observation of popular attitudes and beliefs so that popular opinion could be properly understood. If there was a unity of vision, there was an immediate parting of the ways concerning research. Tom Harrisson based himself in Davenport Street in Bolton to establish the *Worktown* project. Charles Madge and Humphrey Jennings set up the collation of observers' diaries in Blackheath.

Madge and Jennings recruited some 500 volunteers from the general public to form what they called *"a national panel."* The panel were asked to record the every day concerns of their lives on the twelfth of each month, including dreams, hopes, and fears. From time to time they were also asked to write a report or comment on a specific topic such as "Royalty" and to help with the completion of questionnaires. This activity produced the first full-scale book by Mass-Observation - *May 12th* - providing reactions the coronation of George VI and accounts of what the panel thought and did on that day. The book received a mixed reception, with Evelyn Waugh accusing it of *"pseudo-scientific showmanship"* but the evidence gathered is invaluable and can be used to analyse popular views on royalty, the abdication crisis and the role of the King as the country approached war.

At the same time Harrisson's team of investigators produced a documentary account of everyday life in Bolton and Blackpool by observing, talking to and recording the views and activities of people from all levels of society. They analysed religious occasions such as weddings, christenings and funerals, as an anthropologist would analyse ritual behaviour. They attended political and social meetings, sporting and leisure activities, and observed and interviewed their subjects in the street and at work. Although the recordings of the investigators were sometimes subjective, the observations revealed a level of public feeling which went beyond the direct expression of an opinion.

The *Worktown* project collected an astonishing amount of material, but very little was published. One aspect (concerning seaside music hall jokes) appears in Mass-Observation's *First Year's Work* (1938), an upbeat summary of their progress to date, to which Malinowski contributed an essay.

Two more books co-authored by Madge and Harrisson served to establish the reputation of Mass-Observation. These were *Britain by Mass-Observation* (1939) and *War Begins at Home* (1940). The former was an analysis of public opinion at the time of the Munich crisis and drew heavily on fieldwork and diarists' accounts. It looked at the ways in which Hitler and Chamberlain were presented as mythical figures, evil incarnate and the magical bringer of peace, and at the methods by which politicians and the press sought to sway popular views. It showed that the Press was out of step in its hero-worship of Chamberlain as the public had seen through the Prime Minister from the time of the second Munich meeting and the abandonment of Czechoslovakia.

War Begins at Home was similarly critical of the Chamberlain government which was disparaged as being completely out of touch with the views of the public during the first months of war, as it had been during the period of appeasement with Germany.

The outbreak of war inevitably disrupted the activities of Mass-Observation and accelerated the divisions that were growing among its founders. Humphrey Jennings left in 1938 to join the Crown Film Unit. Charles Madge left in mid-1940 to oversee a wartime research project for the Institute of Economic and Social Research on *Wartime Patterns of Saving and Spending.* All activities were centralised in London and Tom Harrisson took over direction of the work.

Madge did not agree with Harrisson that Mass-Observation should accept the patronage of the Ministry of Information during the war (even though it was offered by a good friend, Dick Crossman). He was worried that they would become an instrument of propaganda and a part of the establishment. Harrisson saw this as a unique opportunity to gather facts on popular opinion *"so that after the war we may be able to tell the truth for the first time."* It was also a means to keep Mass-Observation going. The work in Bolton was suspended in 1940 and the panel of diarists were asked to respond to monthly directives asking their opinions on subjects such as air raids, black-outs, employment and rationing. There were daily records of people's reactions to the news and special investigations on subjects such as the response to the bombing of Coventry in November 1940. These surveys provided the basis of Mass-Observation's *Weekly Intelligence Reports* for the Ministry of Information, and also for their reports for individual companies relating to shopping and lifestyles. As always, Mass-Observation were careful to retain the original evidence wherever possible so that it could be subjected to subsequent analysis free from the methodologies and preoccupations of the day.

Tom Harrisson joined the army late in 1942. After a year at a Yorkshire training camp where he devoted his free time to overseeing the publication of *The Pub and the People: a Worktown Study* (1943), he was parachuted into Borneo as a member of the covert Special Operations Executive (SOE). Until his return in 1946, another full time Observer, Bob Willcock, took over control of Mass-Observation. Writing in 1943 in the *American Journal of Sociology* Willcock noted that:

"Mass-Observation is particularly concerned with people's behaviour, their subjective feelings, their worries, frustrations, hopes, desires and fears ... The Blitz period, despite and even partly because of its human tragedies, was a field day for Mass-Observation."

Willcock helped to organise surveys of factory life, fashion, radio, religion, films and hundreds of other topics. Mass-Observation also played a major role in sounding out public opinion regarding the post war world and the need for social reform. As well as surveys on the Beveridge Report, there were numerous studies on issues such as Reconstruction, Health, Education, Demobilisation, Fuel, Food and Housing.

After the war Mass-Observation continued to function as a hybrid between a gatherer of public opinion for the government and a market research analyst. In 1947 Willcock left to work directly for the British Social Survey Unit and Tom Harrisson accepted a post as Government Ethnologist for Sarawak. In 1949 Harrisson passed his rights over to Mass-Observation (UK) Ltd, an independent market research organisation, that continues today as a subsidiary of the British Market Research Bureau. In exchange he retained all rights to the pre-1949 material which was deposited at the University of Sussex in 1970 at the invitation of Asa Briggs, then Vice-Chancellor at Sussex. This material was subsequently deeded to the university in 1975.

During his return to Britain in 1959 Tom Harrisson presided over a second visit to Bolton and Blackpool and papers relating to this are also in the archive. In 1975 he started a further project on attitudes towards royalty. Sadly the untimely death of Tom Harrisson and his wife in a motor accident in Bangkok halted this, but the work was completed by Philip Ziegler. A further phase of Mass-Observation activity was started by Dorothy Sheridan with *Mass-Observation in the 1980s* and has continued through the 1990s and into the new millennium with the assistance of a new panel of volunteers.

The Mass-Observation Archive was officially opened at the University of Sussex in 1975 and offers access to all of this material. The papers of the Mass-Observation can be divided into seven groups:

- **Publications**, 1937-continuing - Twenty-five books appeared during Mass-Observation's original phase of activity, 1937-1950, most of which are now out of print. Two further books were published in the 1960s and Mass-Observation has generated over a dozen more since 1981, as well as booklets for schools.
- **The Worktown Collection,** 1937-1940 - these are the sixty-five boxes of material gathered during Mass-Observation's first major field survey.
- **The Topic Collections**, 1937-1960 - the primary material generated by Mass-Observation's studies on a host of topics from 1937 onwards including records of interviews, detailed questionnaires, written submissions from observers and ephemera related to the topic.
- **The File Reports**, 1937-1972 - these are the typewritten reports which summarised their investigations. These are a very useful introduction to the boxed collections and particularly to the Topic Collections.
- **The Day Surveys**, 1937-1938 - these were the diaries kept by the 500 strong panel on the 12th of each month.
- **The Diaries,** 1939-1963 - Even after the discontinuation of the Day Surveys many observers continued to submit a monthly diary to Mass-Observation. Not all are complete and many diarists stopped writing after the war. The latest diary submitted was in 1963. *Nella Last's War* and *Among You Taking Notes* were based on the Diaries.
- **The Directive Replies**, 1939-1955 - over 3,000 people responded to the monthly questionnaires sent out by Mass-Observation concerning race, class, marriage, money, health, education and other topics.

The Mass-Observation Archive also includes material generated by the new panel of volunteer writers since 1981. It continues to place an emphasis on subjective experience and descriptively rich material which can offer insights into every day life. This qualitative data is complementary to the data derived from statistical and quantitative social research.

Adam Matthew Publications is delighted to be working with the Mass-Observation Archive at the University of Sussex to make the original research notes, records and publications more widely available. The microfilm edition is divided into a number of parts.

Part 1: Publications, 1937-1966

Part One of the microfilm publication acts as an introduction to the archive consisting of all twenty-five books published by Mass-Observation during its initial period of activity from 1937 to 1950, both books published in the 1960s and a guide to the archives. Few libraries possess these volumes and most are out of print. They are used heavily by researchers at the archive as they offer carefully worked analysis of projects undertaken by Mass-Observation. Titles include:

- *Mass-Observation* (1937) - a general introduction by Charles Madge and Tom Harrisson;
- Early publications such as *May 12th: Mass-Observation Day Surveys* (1937); *First Year's Work* (1938); *Britain by Mass-Observation* (1939); *War Begins at Home*, (1940);
- Copies of *Weekly Intelligence Service* issued February - May 1940
- Reports on *Clothes Rationing* (1941), *Home Propaganda* (1941), *A Savings Survey* (1941), *People in Production* (1942) *People's Homes* (1942) and *The Journey Home* (1944);
- *War Factory* (1943) and *The Pub and the People* (1943);
- Individual surveys such as *An Exmoor Village* (1947) and *Browns of Chester* (a shop survey, 1947);
- Reports on social and political issues such as *Britain and her Birth-rate* (1945), *Peace and the Public* (1947), *Juvenile Delinquency* (1948), *The Press and its Readers* (1949) and *Vote's Choice* (1950).

We also include both volumes that appeared between the formation of Mass-Observation (UK) Ltd in 1949 and the establishment of the Archive at the University of Sussex in 1970. These have also been long out of print. They are *Britain Revisited,* (1961) by Tom Harrisson and *Long to Reign Over Us,* (1966) by William Kimber.

These volumes are essential reading for anyone interested in the Mass-Observation project and their wide-ranging sociological investigations of British life from 1937 to 1966. They will be welcomed by anthropologists, social scientists and cultural historians.

Parts 2 & 3: The Worktown Collection, 1937-1940

Mass-Observation's first major study was of a typical northern industrial town (a *Worktown*). They chose Bolton because of *"what it shares in common with other principal working-class and industrial work places throughout Britain."* But to get a full picture of people's lives they also had to study Blackpool (*Holidaytown*) where so many of the local people took their annual holiday.

The team of investigators, led by Harrisson, was made up of students, artists and writers, photographers, unemployed workers and local people. At peak periods (during university vacations) there were up to 60 investigators and the project was run from a base at 85 Davenport Street, Bolton.

All aspects of life and society were observed and recorded, just as if they were making notes on Trobriand Islanders. They explored rituals ranging from religious services to evenings at the pub. They charted beliefs, noting the activities of communist supporters of the Spanish Civil War, Fascist sympathisers of Hitler, and more traditional middle of the road views. They recorded urban myths, rude stories, jokes and graffiti. They studied class behaviour and the structure of society.

They achieved all this by following their subjects everywhere. At home, in the bed-sit, going to work on the bus, in the factory, in shops, in cafes, at football matches, in chip shops, at the cinema and on holiday. There is material on by-elections, jumble sales, the Boys' Brigade, household budgets, public houses, pets, dances, jazz, education, shopping, children and food. Tom Harrisson reflected in 1970: *"We sought to fully penetrate the society we were studying , to live in it as effective members of it and to percolate into every corner of every day and every night..."*

The evidence and analysis gathered fills 65 archival boxes containing nearly 40,000 pages of original notes. In addition to material gathered between 1937 and 1940, there are notes made when they revisited the sites in 1960. All files have been filmed in their entirety.

The Worktown Collection contains excellent source material for all those interested in studying the ordinary people of Britain during a period of great change. It is a vital research tool for social historians, labour historians, historians of leisure, sociologists, and to those studying the fiction of Bennett, Lawrence and Orwell.

Parts 4-8: Topic Collections

There are over 80 Topic Collections in the Mass-Observation Archive at the University of Sussex covering issues as diverse as Adult & Higher Education; Air Raids; Anti-Semitism; Beveridge Report Surveys; Commodities; Drinking Habits; Happiness; Housing; Leisure; Personal Appearance and Clothes; Reconstruction; Sexual Behaviour; Shopping; Work and Youth. These represent surveys and investigations carried out by Mass-Observation mainly between 1937 and 1949, with some later files for the 1960s and 1970s.

Together with the Worktown Collection these represent the raw material of the Mass-Observation Archive. Some of this was worked up into a polished form in the Publications which appear in Part 1 of this series. Brief details also appeared in the File Reports, some of which have been published in microfiche. But this is the first time that Topic Collections have been published in their entirety, giving scholars an opportunity to re-examine and re-interpret the data.

The material to be found in *The Topic Collections* includes not only accounts of interviews but also descriptions of people, places and events, reports with drafts and plans for proposed books, project plans, instructions to investigators, questionnaire replies, internal memoranda, correspondence, printed booklets, photographs, graphs and diagrams, maps, posters, tickets, bills, advertisements and press cuttings. It is indispensable to the researcher who wishes to study the unfiltered views of the "man in the street" with regard to all kinds of contemporary issues and gives an insight into public feeling captured through a qualitative method of approach.

Part 4: Topic Collections on Social Welfare and the Beveridge Report, 1939-1949

Part 4 covers eight Topic Collections which have a strong bearing on Social Welfare and the Beveridge Report. These are:

- ★ Reconstruction
- ★ Family Planning
- ★ Health
- ★ Day Nurseries
- ★ Adult and Higher Education
- ★ Post War Hopes
- ★ Public Administration/Social Services
- ★ Beveridge Report Surveys.

Some consist of a single box, others run to up to six boxes. All comprise individually lettered files within the boxes, all of which have been filmed in their entirety.

Their aim is set out in one of the early Reconstruction files (TC2/2/D): *"The central aim of what we are doing is to find out what people really feel about events after the war, what their private hopes and fears are about their homes, their jobs, the political mechanism designed to make their wants known, as distinct from what planners, politicians and press-men would like them to feel."*

This material will be invaluable to anyone interested in social welfare. The Topic Collections offer a unique grass roots perspective of these issues, offering the genuine views of the public, rather than the wishes of the planners and politicians. The files will be used by historians trying to understand the Labour landslide of 1945, by sociologists and social historians investigating cultural issues, and by those studying Family Planning, Post War Reconstruction and State Provision for Social Need.

Part 5: Topic Collections on Welfare and Social Conditions, 1939-1949

Part 5 continues coverage of welfare related topics with collections on:

★ Housing, 1938-1948 (TC1, 10 boxes)
★ Work: Registration & Demobilisation, 1939-1946 (TC27, 3 boxes)
★ Food, 1937-1952 (TC67, 9 boxes)
★ Fuel, 1937-1947 (TC68, 5 boxes)

The scope of the Housing files is remarkably wide and embraces a number of the key themes of social history. Where did people live their lives? How did they live their lives? What was the social geography of the home? What did people think about their homes? All of these issues are addressed.

The files on Work deal principally with Unemployment and Demobilisation. The starting point is a survey of unemployment in 1939 and an account of contemporary demonstrations. By 1941, following conscription and national service, the emphasis had changed. In a survey carried out in 1942 one man was asked: "What do you think will happen to the men who are demobilised after the war?" His answer was phlegmatic: *"They'll all be put in the queue for the dole and forgotten."*

World War II was as much an economic war as a military one as is revealed on the files on Food and Fuel. Attacks on convoys, disruption of shipping and concentration on rearmament and the war effort resulted in food and fuel shortages at home. Rationing started as early as 1940 and continued until 1950 as Britain's ruined economy struggled to cope with post-war realities. There are also illustrations of Mass-Observation's forays into market research with research exercises carried out regarding margarine, coffee, fish fillets and crisp-bread.

Housing, Work, Food and Fuel are all key areas for any analysis of welfare and social conditions during and after World War II. They help to explain the desire for home ownership, the interest in gardening, and the need to build a 'New Britain' after the war.

Part 6: Topic Collections - The Home Front During World War Two

The experience of war is the focus of Part 6 with Topic Collections covering:

★ Evacuation, 1939-1944 (TC5, 2 boxes)
★ Youth, 1937-1943 (TC51, 3 boxes)
★ Children & Education, 1932-1952 (TC59, 7 boxes)
★ Women in Wartime, 1939-1945 (TC32, 4 boxes)
★ Anti-Semitism, 1939-1951 (TC62, 4 boxes)

The first three of these Topic Collections concentrate on the experience of children before, during and after World War II. These provide a unique perspective on events. For instance, Box 4 of the Children & Education series contains hundreds of essays written by children in 1937 describing *"The Finest Man Who Ever Lived."* King George V is the most popular choice, which is perhaps indicative of patriotic fervour, but Edward VIII, Gandhi, Haile Selassie, Hitler (*"He has raised a nation from the dust and made it a first rate power"*) and even Raymond Westwood (inside-left for Bolton Wanderers) are chosen.

The joys and horrors of evacuation are told by children in their own words and the problems of maintaining good quality education in constrained circumstances is revealed by many teachers who responded to Mass-Observation's surveys. There are also accounts of the war-time reading habits of children, including an analysis of some comics from 1940.

As Penny Summerfield has noted *"Mass-Observation is a major source for social historians writing about women and work in the second world war"* (*PRAXIS* 37/38) and the collection dealing with Women in Wartime is one of their most important groups of material relating to this topic. Much of the evidence concerns an investigation into wartime employment for women resulting from the ATS (Auxiliary Territorial Service) survey of 1941. This reveals women's attitudes to work and documents their experiences in the Land Army, in telephone exchanges, in war factories, in the WAAF and in other fields of employment open to women.

Finally, the Topic Collection relating to Anti-Semitism reveals attitudes to Jews in Britain in 1939, 1946-1947 and 1951. The 1939 survey of London's East End is particularly revealing and capture the views of ordinary people in their own words. The later surveys show how views changed following the discovery of the death camps and terrorist activity (aimed at British soldiers) in Palestine. The answers to the question—*"How do you feel about what's going on in Palestine?"* - are extremely interesting.

Part 7: Topic Collections - Air-Raids, Morale and the Blitz

This seventh part continues coverage of Topic Collections relating to the Home Front During World War II. It covers:

- ★ Air-Raids, 1938-1945 (TC23, 12 boxes)
- ★ Propaganda and Morale, 1939-1944 (TC43, 5 boxes)
- ★ London Survey, 1940 (TC65, 5 boxes)

There is exceptional material on the Blitz, with first-hand accounts of air-raids, descriptions of the devastation caused and the impact that this had on those concerned. London was not alone in sustaining damage and there is also extensive coverage of air-raids across the country, from Aberdeen to Brighton, and from Cardiff to Coventry. There is material on the preparations that were made for the raids and the reparations that followed them. There is much on the ARP and fire services and on the building of shelters. Above all, these papers capture the experience of ordinary people caught up in the war. The following extracts give a flavour of the material:

"A group of six men were looking quietly at the Cathedral ruins. They said little, but 'awful' and 'terrible' were words they applied to the scene. When one middle-aged man remarked 'And this is the Twentieth Century,' he probably epitomised the feelings of the whole group."
(TC23, Box 8, File T: Description of the aftermath of a raid on Coventry).

"Don't remember when a.r. warning went: was enlarging Joyce's portraits ... went from dark room to scullery to examine in light. Heard what sounded like cannon (machine cannon which had heard before during dog-fights over town). As stood at door opening to yard, 'cannon fire' very loud: heard some

things falling & thinking these might be empty shells, went in - as did so heard bangs definitely very loud and close, quickly land on face on scullery floor & put head under sink - another bang. Heard more stuff coming down - glass and rubble ...." (TC23, Box 8, File G: Description of air-raid over Brighton).

"The village of Radlett is not more than twenty miles from London. But the impression that many people have is that London is razed to the ground, 'crucified' as a waiter said. One lady living in St John's Wood won't risk even going back for a day to her house, another refuses to visit her house in Kensington. Apparently part of this scare had been caused by a lady from Golders Green who had produced some very vivid stories." (TC65 Box 4, File A).

"[I] got the impression that people whose homes are <u>completely</u> destroyed seem to have a more carefree attitude to the whole situation, and to be much more optimistic and full of plans, than those whose homes were only partially damaged - windows broken, etc. A woman who has kept a little shop and finds it reduced to a heap of rubble would display quite an amount of gaiety and joking good humour about it, while one whose windows had been blown in and spoilt the current load of goods tended to be just miserable, and sometimes full of grievances about compensation etc (about which there seems to be almost total ignorance and many rumours on all hands). It seemed that total destruction brings with it a sense of relief from responsibility." (TC23, Box 7, File A).

Topic Collection 43 (Propaganda & Morale) looks at the psychological impact of the bombing campaign and also at a wider range of issues such as attitudes towards Evacuation, Jews, War Aims and the like. In Tom Harrisson's words: *"It's value is that it tells us exhaustively about the lower professional group (shopkeepers, clerks, civil servants) who probably dominate the country numerically and otherwise."*

<u>Part 8: Topic Collections - Conscription, Pacifism and War Service</u>

Part 8 covers four further topic collections relating to World War II.

★ Conscientious Objection and Pacifism, 1939-1944 (TC6, 3 boxes)
★ Forces (Men), 1939-1956 (TC29, 5 boxes)
★ Gas Masks, 1939-1943 (TC55, 2 boxes)
★ Dogs in Wartime, 1939-1942 (TC79, 1 box)

It explores the war time experiences of those who served during the war and those who chose not to.

During World War II there were over 40,000 conscientious objectors in Britain. Most were from middle and lower-middle class backgrounds and were influenced by religious beliefs. TC6 explores their experience of the war, mainly through individual accounts sent in by members of the Mass-Observation panel who were either C.O.'s or involved in pacifist activities. The papers document the attitudes of others towards them:

"To the conventionally minded some of them look odd and arty. ... [With] a tendency to be vegetarian, love their mothers, and love animals."

There are many descriptions of pacifist meetings and the violent antagonism that these sometimes engendered.

The section on Forces (TC29) covers a wide range of material including personal reports from male volunteer Mass-Observers in the Armed Forces; the Conscription Survey (1939); views on recruitment (1939); thoughts on Army Education; and attitudes of the public towards the forces (1940-41):

"For a long time I felt sorry for [soldiers], pitied them, their lives were just being thrown away. But I feel rather different now and I envy them a bit because their minds are made up, they have no doubts as to whether what they are doing is right or whether they are doing the right thing. I still feel sorry for them, their lives have been messed up, especially those about 26 or 27 who have made their names and have got to give it all up without any real reward. The only thing I do not feel is pride in them, because their very existence shows what a hell of a position we're in." (TC29, Box 1, File F)

There is much on life in the Forces, including soldier's views of the Blitz, the conduct of the war, army training and on fellow combatants (there was fierce rivalry - even hostility - between many allied forces).

Material on the 'Home Guard' shows the intense seriousness and, at the same time, ludicrousness of Britain's attempts to repel potential invaders. Scholars will welcome the inclusion of many posters and booklets dispensing government advice, contrasted with accounts of military manoeuvres and training facilities by volunteers themselves.

The section on Gas Masks looks at provides a detailed survey of government instructions and advice about gas masks and the extent to which this was taken up by the general public. The carrying of gas masks by civilians also came to be seen as a key indicator of wartime morale.

Public attitudes to dogs in wartime are analysed in TC79. Should they be evacuated? Could Britain afford to feed them when all food was rationed and even bones were recycled for human consumption in broth? How did dogs cope with air raids? There are also comments on various wartime accessories for dogs: *"gas masks for domestic dogs or cats are, in our experience, quite impractical..."* The value of dogs for companionship was balanced with the practical issues of keeping them.

For the social historian, these sources will allow a more detailed and interesting account of everyday wartime experience to be compiled.

William Pidduck
September 2005

Acknowledgements

Thanks are due to Dorothy Sheridan, Fiona Courage, Joy Eldridge and Helen Monk at the Mass-Observation Archive for their help in the preparation of this microfilm edition. This brief account of Mass-Observation and its papers has been largely based on:

Dorothy Sheridan, *The Tom Harrisson Mass-Observation Archive: A Guide for Researchers,* University of Sussex Library, October 1995 (Revised)

and

Tom Jeffery, *Mass-Observation: A short history,* Mass-Observation Occasional Paper No 10, University of Sussex Library, 1999 (new edition)

Further details concerning Mass-Observation, the Archive, and publications available for purchase can be found on the Mass-Observation website at:

http://www.sussex.ac.uk/library/massobs

INTRODUCTION TO THE TOPIC COLLECTIONS
BY DOROTHY SHERIDAN

The primary material generated by Mass-Observation's studies from 1937 onwards have been grouped together by subject matter in Topic Collections (TCs). Although every effort has been made to retain the original arrangement of the material and keep all the papers relating to one study together, the groups are to some extent artificial, especially where several years are spanned within a single TC. In most cases, every TC contains the papers resulting from one or two major studies but other papers which are closely related have been included. It has been very difficult to reconstruct an original order with these papers because Mass-Observation itself over the years re-arranged material, and annotated older papers when repeating a study years later. In some cases, unfortunately, papers from the same main study can be found in separate TCs. Please note, however, that the full handlists can be searched electronically for key words and phrases.

The boxes contain a range of forms of material: reports, drafts of reports and plans for proposed books, descriptions of people, places and events, accounts of interviews, project plans, instructions to investigators, questionnaire replies, internal memoranda, correspondence, printed booklets, photographs, graphs and diagrams, maps, posters, tickets, bills, advertisements and press cuttings. The Topic Collections are predominantly the work of paid fuller part-time investigators, and do not normally include material sent in by the volunteer panel. However, where diaries and directive replies have been analysed for inclusion in a particular study, typed extracts from panel material may be found.

Links to the publications and the Files Report sequence

The relationship between the File Reports and the Topic Collections is close but not exactly parallel. Not all studies were written up as File Reports or books. In some cases, the primary material behind a study has not survived. There is no system of cross reference, but handlists for both groups of papers may be searched electronically.

Codes and abbreviations

De-coding Mass-Observation's symbols, abbreviations and terminology is a creative task and the key offered here should be taken as guidance only. Over the years, different members of the M-O team used different systems of recording.

"Directs":	responses on a theme elicited directly by M-O investigators from members of the public
"Indirects"	responses on a theme elicited by a M-O investigators in the course of an informal conversation with a member of the public
"Overheards"	snatches of conversation gathered by a M-O investigators without the person being aware of being recorded
"Follows"	descriptions of a person's behaviour while being followed by a M-O investigator (used mostly in pre-war work)

A simple system of coding was used for visual identification of social class:

A	"Rich people"
B	"The Middle Classes"
C	"Artisans and skilled workers"
D	"Unskilled workers and the least economically or educationally trained of our people"

Thus "F30B" refers to a thirty year old middle class woman (F=female) and "M20D" refers to a twenty-year old unskilled man. This code is listed at the beginning of the M-O publication *War Factory* (1943).

Initials with the date at the top of a page usually refer to the M-O investigator (or "Inv") who wrote the report or carried out the interview.

Referencing items from the Topic Collections in publications

Cite the Topic Collection title, followed by the box number and file letter.
Example:

M-OA: TC Air Raids, 3/C
You can add further details as follows: e.g. Observation in an air raid shelter, Sept 1940.

The Topic Collection numbers

There is no significance to the numbering given to the Topic Collections. Each Topic Collection was allocated a number as it was sorted and listed.

Topic Collections by number

TC	Topic	
1	Housing 1938-48	*Pt 5
2	Reconstruction 1941-43	*Pt 4
3	Family Planning 1944-49	*Pt 4
4	Shopping 1939-63	
5	Evacuation 1939-44	*Pt 6
6	Conscientious Objection & Pacifism 1939-44	*Pt 8
7	Happiness 1938	
8	Astrology and Spiritualism 1938-47	
9	Korea 1950	
10	Labour Party Campaign "Ask Your Dad" 1948	
11	Juvenile Delinquency 1946-47	
12	Sexual Behaviour 1939-50	
13	Health 1939-49	*Pt 4
14	Famous Persons 1938-52	
15	Demolition in London 1941	
16	Live Entertainment 1938-48	
17	Films 1937-48	
18	Personal Appearance and Clothes 1938-54	
19	Day Nurseries 1941-46	*Pt 4
20	Reading Habits 1937-47	
21	Co-operative Stores 1939-47	
22	Commercial Advertising 1938-47	
23	Air Raids 1938-45	*Pt 7
24	Browns of Chester 1942-55	
25	Political Attitudes & Behaviour 1938-56	
26	"Britain Can Make It" Exhibition 1946	
27	Work: Registration and Demobilisation 1938-46	*Pt 5
28	Dreams 1937-48	
29	Forces (Men) 1939-56	*Pt 8

30	Bird-Nesting 1951	
31	Blind People 1947	
32	Women in Wartime 1939-45	*Pt 6
33	Art 1938-49	
34	Science 1938-47	
35	Air Raid Shelter Competition 1939	
36	Adult and Higher Education 1937-48	*Pt 4
37	Magazines 1940-53	
38	Music, Dancing & Jazz 1939-41	
39	Picture Postcard Analysis 1940-41	
40	Post War Hopes 1944	*Pt 4
41	Games & Jigsaws 1937-41	
42	Posters 1939-47	
43	Propaganda & Morale 1939-44	*Pt 7
44	Public Administration & Social Services in Wartime 1941-42	*Pt 4
45	Radio Rediffusion Surveys 1949 & 1955	
46	By-Elections 1937-47	
47	Religion 1937-50	
48	Squatting 1946	
49	Victory Celebrations 1945-46	
50	World Outlook 1945-50	
51	Youth 1937-43	*Pt 6
52	Photography 1940-44	
53	Beveridge Report Surveys 1942-47	*Pt 4
54	Police, Law and Invasion Preparations 1939-41	
55	Gas Masks 1939-43	*Pt 8
56	Peace and the Public Survey 1956	
57	The Budget, Money Matters & Household Budgeting 1939-50	
58	Holidays 1937-51	
59	Children & Education 1937-52	*Pt 6
60	Press 1938-42	
61	Newspaper Reading 1937-62	
62	Anti-Semitism 1939-51	*Pt 6
63	Smoking Habits 1937-65	
64	Coal Mining 1938-48	
65	London Survey 1940	*Pt 7
66	Town & District Surveys 1938-49	
67	Food 1937-53	*Pt 5
68	Fuel 1937-47	*Pt 5

69 Royalty 1937-60
70 Transport 1937-43 and 1963
71 Road Safety 1946-55
72 Capital Punishment 1938-56
73 Poetry 1939-40
74 Radio Listening 1939-48
75 Industry 1940-55
76 General Elections 1945-55
77 Jokes 1939-47
78 Commodities 1941-64
79 Dogs in Wartime 1939-42 *Pt 8
80 Leisure 1940-47
81 "Meet Yourself on Sunday" 1948-50
82 Sport 1939-47
83 Voting Attitudes 1944
84 Local Council Elections 1937-51
85 Drinking Habits 1939-63
86 Gambling 1937-51 (in preparation)
87 Wall Chalkings 1939-43

Those marked with an asterisk are covered in this microfilm edition of the Mass-Observation Archive.

If you wish to search the listings for all of the Topic Collections (and other sections of the Mass-Observation Archive such as the File Reports), please go to the Mass-Observation Archive web-site at:

http://www.sussex.ac.uk/library/massobs

Putting on gas mask. First position.

At night, masks on; close windows without showing light.

Gas alert while in the street.

Having put on masks take cover.

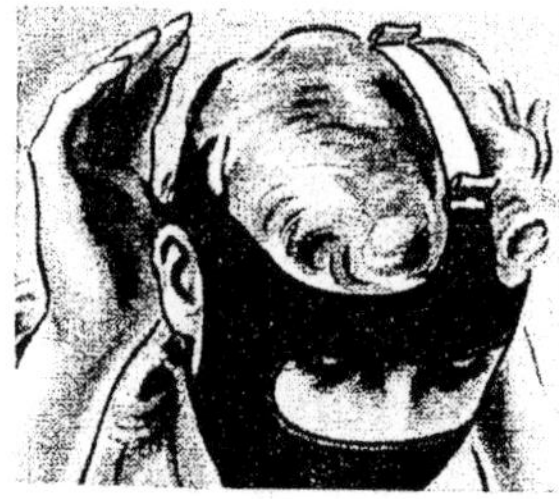

With straps drawn over head.

The facepiece of the gas mask is provided in three standard sizes: small, medium and large. An extra large size is now available for exceptionally large faces. The size is marked on the headstraps or moulded on the brow of the facepiece. The same container is fitted to all types.

The small size of civilian gas mask will fit most children from 4 years upwards as well as some exceptionally developed children under 4 years.

Putting on the gas mask should be a matter of seconds. After a gas alarm the first thing to do is to hold the breath, as it may be dangerous to breathe in before the gas mask is in place. Hat and spectacles or pince-nez must be taken off before the mask is put on, otherwise they may interfere with the fit. Women should see that there are no hair-pins to get in the way, and that the hair is pushed back so that it will not get under the facepiece.

The gas mask should be held in front of the face by each of the side straps, with the thumbs under the straps. The chin should be thrust into the facepiece, and the straps drawn over the head as far as they will reach comfortably. The next thing is to breathe out violently to expel any gas that may have got inside the facepiece; after which normal breathing can be resumed. The hat can then be put on, over the headstraps.

37

Gas masks (TC 23, Box 4)

MASS-OBSERVATION ARCHIVE
PAPERS FROM THE MASS-OBSERVATION ARCHIVE AT THE UNIVERSITY OF SUSSEX
Part 7: Topic Collections - Air-Raids, Morale and the Blitz
(AIR-RAIDS; PROPAGANDA AND MORALE; LONDON SURVEY, 1940)

CONTENTS OF REELS

REEL 117

AIR-RAIDS, 1938-1945 (TC23) Box 1

REEL 118

AIR-RAIDS, 1938-1945 (TC23) Box 2

REEL 119

AIR-RAIDS, 1938-1945 (TC23) Box 3

REEL 120

AIR-RAIDS, 1938-1945 (TC23) Box 4

REEL 121

AIR-RAIDS, 1938-1945 (TC23) Box 5

REEL 122

AIR-RAIDS, 1938-1945 (TC23) Box 6

REEL 123

AIR-RAIDS, 1938-1945 (TC23) Box 7

REEL 124

AIR-RAIDS, 1938-1945 (TC23) Box 8

REEL 125

AIR-RAIDS, 1938-1945 (TC23) Box 9

REEL 126

AIR-RAIDS, 1938-1945 (TC23) Box 10

REEL 127

AIR-RAIDS, 1938-1945 (TC23) Box 11

REEL 128

AIR-RAIDS, 1938-1945 (TC23) Box 12

REEL 129

PROPAGANDA AND MORALE, 1939-1944 (TC43) Box 1

REEL 130

PROPAGANDA AND MORALE, 1939-1944 (TC43) Box 2

REEL 131

PROPAGANDA AND MORALE, 1939-1944 (TC43) Box 3

REEL 132

PROPAGANDA AND MORALE, 1939-1944 (TC43) Box 4

REEL 133

PROPAGANDA AND MORALE, 1939-1944 (TC43) Box 5

REEL 134

LONDON SURVEY, 1940 (TC65) Box 1

REEL 135

LONDON SURVEY, 1940 (TC65) Box 2

REEL 136

LONDON SURVEY, 1940 (TC65) Box 3

REEL 137

LONDON SURVEY, 1940 (TC65) Box 4

REEL 138

LONDON SURVEY, 1940 (TC65) Box 5

FIRE (TC 23, Box 4)

MASS-OBSERVATION ARCHIVE
PAPERS FROM THE MASS-OBSERVATION ARCHIVE
AT THE UNIVERSITY OF SUSSEX
Part 8: Topic Collections - Conscription, Pacifism and War Service
(CONSCIENTIOUS OBJECTION AND PACIFISM; FORCES (MEN);
GAS MASKS; DOGS IN WARTIME)

CONTENTS OF REELS

REEL 139

CONSCIENTIOUS OBJECTION AND PACIFISM, 1939-1944 (TC6) Box 1

REEL 140

CONSCIENTIOUS OBJECTION AND PACIFISM, 1939-1944 (TC6) Box 2

REEL 141

CONSCIENTIOUS OBJECTION AND PACIFISM, 1939-1944 (TC6) Box 3

REEL 142

FORCES (MEN), 1939-1956 (TC29) Box 1

REEL 143

FORCES (MEN), 1939-1956 (TC29) Box 2

REEL 144

FORCES (MEN), 1939-1956 (TC29) Box 3

REEL 145

FORCES (MEN), 1939-1956 (TC29) Box 4

REEL 146

FORCES (MEN), 1939-1956 (TC29) Box 5

REEL 147

GAS MASKS, 1939-1943 (TC55) Box 1

REEL 148

GAS MASKS, 1939-1943 (TC55) Box 2

REEL 149

DOGS IN WARTIME, 1939-1942 (TC79) Box 1

Friends Relief Service (TC 23, Box 4)

AIR RAID PRECAUTIONS

HANDBOOK No. 8

(2nd Edition)

THE DUTIES OF AIR RAID WARDENS

Obtained from
Air Raid Warden

LONDON
HIS MAJESTY'S STATIONERY OFFICE
Price 2d. net

The Duties of Air-Raid Wardens (TC 23, Box 4)

MASS-OBSERVATION ARCHIVE
Papers from the Mass-Observation Archive
at the University of Sussex
Part 7: Topic Collections - Air-Raids, Morale and the Blitz
(AIR-RAIDS; PROPAGANDA AND MORALE; LONDON SURVEY, 1940)

DETAILED LISTING

REEL 117

AIR-RAIDS, 1938-1945

TC23: 12 boxes

TC 23, BOX 1 : 1938-39: PREPARATIONS FOR WAR, THE CRISIS, OUTBREAK OF WAR AND THE FIRST FEW MONTHS

23/1/A: Investigation into ARP
"The Sociology of the ARP " by Mass-Observation in *New Statesman and Nation*, 5.11.38
Newscutting : "What people think of ARP" by Mass-Observation, *Daily Herald*, 17.1.39
Letter from *Daily Herald* to Tom Harrisson re above article
Newscutting : "Deep Shelters Are Not Ruled Out", *News Chronicle*, 10.1.39
Questionnaire on ARP and underground shelters - various replies gathered by Observers AH. and LT. in London areas
Casual interviews in ARP, Bolton
Questionnaire : "What led you to join ARP or NFS. ?" Two pages of extracts from replies, with analyses
Bookmark

Extract:
"Inv heard early in the morning that a house in which his aunt's mother lived had been hit. He went to the road and found this was true. He tried to find

out from the policeman on duty whether there had been any casualties, but the policeman did not know; nor did the rescue party clearing up the mess.

Inv then went to the warden's post; discovered that it was the wrong sector, but was given the information that there had been casualties. Went to the right warden's post where he found that the lady in question had been taken away suffering from shock..."

23/1/B: The Crisis, August - September 1939
Observations at Victoria Station 26.8.39
Informal interviews, overheard comments and observations by JA in various London areas
Count of gas masks being carried, 13.9.39
Assorted oddments, conversations on the impact of the declaration of war

23/1/C: Behaviour during the blackout, September 1939
Observations made in various parts of London by three Observers (JA, WRL. and AH) who followed members of the public through the streets
Two letters to Tom Harrisson from people who had carried out "follows"
Notes on the "follows" with analyses

23/1/D: Reactions to the blackout, September - November 1939
Selected comments taken from Panel material and overheard comments in Bolton
Descriptions of incidents and conversations relating to the blackout
Effects of the blackout on leisure activities : dancing, cinemas, cafes, shops, colleges, sport, parks
Light counts September - November 1939 in London
Observations and accounts of conversations made on the underground and on the main line trains, October 1939 by NM
Cuttings and typed extracts from the press on the blackout, ARP, the progress of the war, October-November 1939

23/1/E: Preparations for air raids, August 1939
Questionnaire survey carried out in Hampstead asking people about blackout preparations, shelters, air raid alarms etc. (45 interviews)
Typed report of conversation with the Deputy Town Clerk of Finchley about the building of shelters, 30.8.39 (TH)

23/1/F: Opinion about the likelihood of air raids on London, October - November 1939

Questionnaire survey carried out at intervals in different types of areas
Report by CF. and qq replies
Questionnaires on the news, December 1939

23/1/G: Detailed observations of community life at the outbreak of war, September 1939
Letter and report by DMH. at Sidford, South Devon
Letter and report by BA at Glenfield, Leicestershire

23/1/H: Effects of the outbreak of war on ordinary life
Personal letters :
To Tom Harrisson from his mother in Winchester, August 1939
To Tom Harrisson from his wife Biddy (Clayton) in West Stafford, Dorset
To Tom Harrisson and Biddy from her mother, Elinor Pellatt, in Dorset
To Elinor Pellatt, from Mary Clayton (Biddy Clayton's first mother-in-law)
[Tom Harrisson married Biddy Clayton née Pellatt. Biddy's first husband was Michael Clayton and they had a son, John, aged about six in 1939]
To unknown person from Lady Anne Hill
Observations by Tom Harrisson, August - September 1939. Accounts of journey from London to Dorchester. Account of visit to mother-in-law's home, Dorset

23/1/I: Accounts of volunteer stretcher bearers
Report : Hampstead Rescue Party Depot 3 [stretcher bearers], HDW., September 1939
Report : Observers' experiences : ARP, Ealing, WRL, December 1939

Reactions to officials
Extracts from panel material referring to ARP wardens, 1939
Report on ARP wardens, Streatham, by Observer WP, September 1939
Observation of a war policeman on duty, West Ealing, September 1939
Report on the vigilance of ARP officials in Harrow, by CLB., September 1939
Reactions to the sound of the air raid siren, August - November 1939
Reactions to air raid warning and sight of German bomber in Bolton, November 1939
Assorted notes and observations on ARP

23/1/J: Shelters in Fulham, November 1939
Report by Observer KB on the state of Anderson shelters
Extract:
"Obs saw 16 shelters, and collected about 20 opinions on them. Most of the

REEL 117, TC 23, BOX 1 (continued)

shelters had been sandbagged in front of the entrance and some all round. Most had boarded floors and many had put down lino or pieces of old carpet ....The favourite form of lighting was a candle ....

Generally people seem quite pleased with the shelters saying they will at any rate give protection from shrapnel and splinters .... The chief complaint was that people would have to get out of their warm beds and go out in the cold to them, thus making illness. "If you have to either die of pneumonia or get bombed, I don't know which is worst."

Another complaint from some people was that the shelters were very damp. One woman had toad-stools growing inside hers ...."

REEL 118

TC 23, BOX 2 : FULHAM ARP STUDY 1939 I

23/2/A: Attitudes to the ARP in Fulham, March 1939
63 Questionnaire replies to 4 questions on what people think of the local ARP, whether the Council is doing its best, whether Fulham is prepared for war and interviewees' own voluntary efforts. KB

23/2/B: Opinions of ARP volunteers in Fulham, April 1939.
50 interviews with volunteers about why they offered their services and what factors influenced their decision. KB (2 copies)

23/2/C Pilot study : ARP volunteers in Fulham, April -May 1939
Copy of questionnaire with 6 questions (as above), with 63 replies (KB) plus a further 8 replies from Observers MR. and LT
Analysis of results

23/2/D: Preliminary survey : ARP volunteers in Fulham, May 1939
Copies of questionnaire (8/9 qqs)
42 replies; interviews by KB, LT, EBC, MER
Brief summary of results by EBC

23/2/E: Personal accounts from ARP volunteers
8 short reports on ARP work sent to KB

23/2/F: ARP in Fulham May - June 1939
Various manuscripts describing Mass-Observation's major study, with sections on method and results, covering recruitment and propaganda, reasons for volunteering and attitudes to ARP work
Notes on ARP propaganda
ARP leaflets

23/2/G: Questionnaire : ARP Study, May 1939
Various drafts with notes by TH and KB

Questionnaire replies, May - June 1939 (Total 769)
23/2/H: From Observers DS (62) and AH (78)
23/2/I: From Observer HAC (116)
23/2/J: From Observer KB (413)
23/2/K: From Observer EBC. (96)
23/2/L: From Observer MER. (134)

REEL 119

TC 23, BOX 3 : FULHAM ARP STUDY, 1939 II

23/3/A: Breakdown of results: Tables and analysis sheets
23/3/B: Tabulation of results
23/3/C: Address labels for ARP volunteers (omitted)
23/3/D: Address list of ARP volunteers (omitted)

REEL 120

TC 23, BOX 4 : PRINTED OFFICIAL MATERIAL

23/4/A: Air Raid Precautions : official advice and information.
Air Raids : What you must do, What you must know. Ministry of Home Security, 1941
Posters: 3 Fougasse posters on ARP
Booklet : *The Duties of an Air Raid Warden.* HMSO, 1938
Selection of leaflets about ARP on home security, recruitment to voluntary services, the ARP card, the ARP button, warden's form for reporting air raid damage
Sudden birth in an air raid shelter: "instructions for persons in charge of air raid shelters...." Ministry of Health, June 1940
[Air Raid Precautions Memo No.16 *Working after the siren.* Ministry of Home

REEL 120, TC 23, BOX 4 (continued)

Security (1940) - moved to Topic Collection INDUSTRY: 6/j]
Note outside a pub: *"No gas; no water; but good spirits."*

23/4/B: ARP social functions
Miscellaneous notes and printed ephemera

23/4/C: ARP magazines
Correspondence between Mass-Observation and the producers of ARP publications, 1940 - 1
Report on ARP magazines (BW 26.7.40)

23/4/D: Gas : protection and advice
Booklets, leaflets, cuttings and posters on the use of gas masks and the identification of types of gas attacks

23/4/E: Commercial ARP products
Selection of advertising material and information booklets produced by commercial firms, including items on protecting the home, types of shelter, useful publications on ARP, blackout etc

23/4/F: Fire watching
Recruiting leaflets for the Auxiliary Fire Service, instructions for dealing with fire bombs, forms for volunteers

23/4/G: First aid
Recruitment leaflets, Red Cross enrolment forms, charity requests from Red Cross, Ministry of Health advice leaflet on first aid

23/4/H: Shelters
Selection of official printed items on shelters

23/4/I: Air raid damage and post-raid relief
Pamphlet : *How to act after a raid*, issued by the Dept of Health for Scotland (3 versions for different areas)
Assorted leaflets and forms with information on rest centres, claims for damages, relief, evacuation etc

23/4/J: Air raids
Cuttings from national and local press, 1940 - 1

23/4/K: Voluntary organisations
Assorted printed material produced by the Air Raid Defence League, the Friends Relief Service, the War Damage Claimants' Association and the National Council of Social Service

23/4/L: Spitfire Funds and salvage
Publicity and requests for support for Spitfire Funds
Items on salvage, waste and rubbish

23/4/M: National Service
Assorted leaflets on recruitment to Civil Defence and the armed forces

REEL 121

TC 23, BOX 5 : PUBLIC REACTIONS TO AIR RAIDS IN LONDON, 1940. USE AND OPINION OF DIFFERENT TYPES OF SHELTERS. OBSERVATIONS OF BEHAVIOUR IN SHELTERS

Public Shelters
Reactions to alarms; use of public shelters; types of shelters and facilities; descriptions of behaviour, dress, morale; accounts of overheard conversations and incidents. Observations made chiefly in London by full-time Mass-Observation investigators; some reports from voluntary observers. For further reports on air raids, see Directive Replies 1940

23/5/A: Observations gathered June - July 1940

23/5/B: Observations gathered August 1940
News Quotas (JS) August 1940

Extract: *"Bombing and gun-fire is taken as a matter of course in every town in the area, except where the bombs actually fall. That is to say that raids, such as yesterday's, are not subject for much comment by the local people in surrounding districts, but do, naturally, become the centre of interest in the town immediately affected. Similarly with rumour – contrary to general assumption, there was much more rumour in Redhill itself, where the damage was done, than in any other towns, where no damage was done."*
South London, 18/8/40

23/5/C: Observations gathered September 1940
File D: Observations gathered October - November 1940

REEL 121, TC 23, BOX 5 (continued)

23/5/E: Tube shelters : observations in the London Underground, September - November 1940
Reports, observations and impressions gathered in the underground shelters : descriptions of behaviour, clothing, noise, food, facilities, police presence and morale

23/5/F: Brick shelters, July 1940
Report on brick shelters with interviews and accounts of people's opinions on safety of shelters. Account of inspection of shelters by Professor JBS Haldane

23/5/G: Types of shelters, September 1940
Results of small survey asking people in London what they think of the shelters they use; questionnaire also on attitudes to bombing and death

23/5/H: Anderson shelters, September 1940
Reports from Observer LE on private shelters, particularly his family's Anderson shelter in Streatham
General note on Anderson shelters in Kilburn

23/5/I: Tilbury shelter, October 1940
Observations made on facilities, behaviour etc
Replies to questions on the Tilbury shelter - smell, food, organisations, charity efforts, first aid

23/5/J: Tube shelter publications, 1940
Note on papers *The Swiss Cottager* and *Piccadilly Gazette* produced by tube shelterers

REEL 122

TC 23, BOX 6 : USE OF SHELTERS; EFFECTS ON PERSONAL LIFE OF AIR RAIDS; SLEEPING AND EATING PATTERNS; EAR PLUG USE; HEALTH AND FIRST AID; MORALE

23/6/A: Personal diary 5.10.40 - 9.10.40
An account by full-time Observer, KB of her trip from Bristol to London, her family home in Wandsworth and her flat in Fulham; includes information of London bomb damage and on people's attitudes. Description of the plight of

friends who had been bombed out

23/6/B: Questionnaire on use of shelters, November 1940

Survey of sleeping habits, choice of sleep-place and opinions on the safety of shelters. Carried out in London areas; Shepherds Bush, Nottinghill Gate, Streatham, Finchley and Kilburn, approx. 200 interviews

Table of results

23/6/C: Household readjustments, October 1940

Small survey by NM and CF on domestic arrangements during air raids, including sleeping patterns, use of shelters, games played, food available, first aid, clothing and so on. Kilburn and Stepney areas

23/6/D: News Quota Survey October 1940

Questions put to people in Kilburn and Streatham about reactions to the latest news, amount of sleep they have been getting, getting out of London and sleeping in the Underground

23/6/E: Sleeping arrangements, August - September 1940

Detailed observations with interviews : bedding arrangements, people's sleep difficulties, shelter facilities etc

Various observations : effects of war on nerves; psychological strain of the bombing

23/6/F: Ear plugs 1940

Sample of ear plugs. Reports on use of ear plugs, including interviews on people's attitudes to them. (Questionnaire includes question on reactions to slogan : "Be like Dad, keep Mum".)

23/6/G: Health and first aid, 1940

Reports, observations and overheard comments on first aid facilities, ambulances, stretcher bearers, reactions to air raids in hospitals, recruitment of medical personnel (pamphlets), sales in chemist shops of ear plugs, first aid kits etc., casualties and funerals of air raid victims

23/6/H: Air raid morale, 1940 - 41

Reports and impressions of the way in which people cope with raids and behaviour in shelters

Printed pamphlet : *Psychological Effects of Air Raids*, by PE Vernon from *The Journal of Abnormal and Social Psychology*, October 1941

Notes on government propaganda directed at people in bombed areas

Newspaper cuttings on raids, 1940 - 1

REEL 122, TC 23, BOX 6 (continued)

23/6/I: Miscellaneous notes and correspondence
Assorted papers relating to ARP, shelters and air raids

REEL 123

TC 23, BOX 7: ARP AND ATTITUDES TO ARP WARDENS; THE EFFECTS OF AIR RAIDS; FEAR OF PARACHUTISTS; LOCAL DEFENCE VOLUNTEERS (LDV); PROSECUTION UNDER THE DEFENCE REGULATIONS; AIRCRAFT PRODUCTION APPEALS

23/7/A: Homelessness, rest centres and communal feeding, September - October 1940
Observations made in heavily blitzed areas of London, including Stepney, Paddington, and Walthamstow. Interviews with people whose homes have been bombed, impressions of morale, comments on post-raid services and availability of information
Official leaflets
Press cuttings on air raid damage
Leaflets of local Tenants' Defence Leagues, etc.

Extract:
"Inv got the impression that people whose homes are completely destroyed seem to have a more carefree attitude to the whole situation, and to be much more optimistic and full of plans, than those whose homes were only partially damaged – windows broken, etc. A woman who has kept a little shop and finds it reduced to a heap of rubble would display quite an amount of gaiety and joking good humour about it, while one whose windows had blown in or spoilt the current lot of goods tended to be just miserable, and sometimes full of grievances about compensation etc (about which these seems to be almost total ignorance and many rumours on all hands). It seemed that total destruction brings with it a sense of relief from responsibility."

23/7/B: Post raid services, October 1940
Press cuttings, leaflets and correspondence
Leaflets from the Air Raid Damage Relief Fund

23/7/C: Quality of life during air raids, October 1940

Selection of letters from friends and relatives to Mass-Observation volunteer panel members: covers all aspects of life during air raids, including evacuation, reactions to news, shelter social life, sleeping habits, inconveniences caused by war conditions. Letters from all over Britain

23/7/D: Effects of air raids on leisure, entertainment and shopping
Assorted notes and observations relating to the effects of blackout on shopping habits, use of cafes, cinemas, libraries, colleges, clothing and fashion trends
Interviews carried out in September 1940 on visiting friends, domestic activities, radio listening, and newspaper reading, games, eating habits

23/7/E: ARP and ARP Wardens 1939 - 40
Impressions and accounts of incidents at wardens' posts including observations on the behaviour of wardens

23/7/F: ARP Questionnaire, June 1940
Report : "The ARP Card and its Effects". Information based on 105 interviews with householders in 4 areas of London about the ARP card distributed by the Ministry of Home Security. The card contained information of local ARP services
Press-cutting re ARP recruitment, *The Star* 10.6.40
ARP questionnaire with replies

23/7/G: Barrage, September 1939 - 40
Reactions to the sound of anti-aircraft guns. Note on blimps (barrage balloons)
Observations of reactions to blimps in Shepherds Bush Green (JA) 14.9.39

23/7/H: German bomber down, 1939 - 40
Report : local response to incident in small village
Report: rumours of an aeroplane being brought down near Romford, sent in by volunteer, 10.9.39

23/7/I: Fear of parachutists, May 1940
Impressions based on indirect interviews about the likelihood of German soldiers landing by parachute

23/7/J: Local Defence Volunteers (LDV), June - September 1940
General reports from Worcester and Fulham

REEL 123, TC 23, BOX 7 (continued)

23/7/K: Appeal for support of munitions and aircraft production, 1940 - 1941
Report on Aluminium Appeal, 15.7.40
Account of an exhibition of Messerschmitt 109 at Croydon, in aid of Croydon "Spitfire" Fund
Assorted notes and reports on appeal funds, War Weapon Weeks, and propaganda including a Spitfire badge

23/7/L: Regulations and offences, 1940
Copy of *Everyman's Guide to the War Regulations*, 1940
Notes on cases of prosecutions under the Defence Regulations from the press, July 1940

REEL 124

TC 23, BOX 8 : AIR RAIDS IN BRITAIN, 1940-41 TOWNS: A - D

Apart from the first file which contains general information about the bombing of provincial towns, the files contain reports, letters, leaflets, official forms and memoranda and other items relating to a specific town or area. Much of this material has been donated to Mass-Observation by members of the volunteer panel, but the main reports come from full-time Mass Observation investigators

- Further material on air raids is filed with the Directive Replies for 1940
- Additional town files which have been added after the first sorting have been interfiled alphabetically (hence C2)

Other information about air raids may be found in the Topic Collection: TOWN AND DISTRICT SURVEYS

23/8/A: Effects of air raids
Report : *The Effect of Air Raids in Great Britain* published by The Economic League (Central Council). Duplicated copy, 1.7.40
Report : *Reactions to Air Raids as Observed by Citizens Advice Bureaux* (Home Intelligence, from Stephen Taylor to Mary Adams), September 1940? References to a number of cities and towns
Report by Lionel Fielder of Ministry of Food who accompanied Tom Harrisson to Southampton, 3.12.40. No title, but discusses reactions of

civilians to bombing. Annotation "Lord Woolton took this to Cabinet"
Report (M-O) *Plan for Survey of Blitzed Town*, 8.1.41. Guidance for Mass Observation investigators (CF)
Report (M-O) : *Re Morale in Blitzes* by JF, 23.3.41. Suggestions for policy changes in reporting on blitzed towns
Report : *Draft Plan (Mark III) for use in emergencies resulting from serious air raiding,* MOI, 18.1.41

23/8/B: Aberdeen (printed material only)
23/8/C: Barrow-in-Furness (printed and duplicated material only)
23/8/C2: Billingshurst, Sussex
23/8/D: Birmingham
23/8/E: Bishop Auckland, Co Durham
23/8/F: Bolton
23/8/G: Bradford

23/8/H: Brighton
Extract:
"Don't remember when a. r. warning went: was enlarging Joyce's portraits and had test-stripped one onto Bromesko, went from dark room to scullery to examine in light. Heard what sounded like cannon (machine cannon which had heard before during dogfights over town). As stood at door opening to yard, 'cannon fire' very loud: heard some things falling and thinking these might be empty shells, went in – as did so heard bangs definitely very loud and close, quickly land on face on scullery floor and put head under sink – another bang. Heard more stuff coming down – glass and rubble …."
Raid on Brighton 14/9/40 3pm

23/8/I: Bristol
23/8/J: Bromley
23/8/K: Campbeltown, Argyllshire
23/8/K2: Cambridge (rest centres)
23/8/L: Cardiff
23/8/M: Caterham
23/8/N: Chelmsford (duplicated material only)
23/8/O: Cheltenham
Extract:
"The gas works received at least one direct hit but the damage is probably not vital. The only other large building was a workhouse. The rest of the damage was done to small working class homes and shops."
Cheltenham, 18/12/40

REEL 124, TC 23, BOX 8 (continued)

23/8/P: Chepstow
23/8/Q: Clacton
23/8/R: Clydeside, including Glasgow
23/8/S: Consett
(poster and correspondence relating to the Citizens Advice Bureau)
23/8/T: Coventry
Extract:
"A group of six men were looking quietly at the cathedral ruins. They said little, but "awful" and "terrible" were words they applied to the scene. When one middle-aged man remarked "and this is the twentieth century," he probably epitomised the feelings of the whole group."
Coventry, 15/11/40

23/8/U: Croydon
23/8/V: Derby
23/8/W: Doncaster

REEL 125

TC 23, BOX 9 : AIR RAIDS IN BRITAIN, 1940-41: TOWNS D - L

23/9/A: Eastbourne
23/9/B: "East Coast Village", Essex
23/9/B2: Exeter
23/9/C: Gateshead
23/9/C2: Great Malvern
23/9/D: Greenock
23/9/D2: Harrow
23/9/E: Hastings
23/9/F: Huddersfield
23/9/F2: Hull
23/9/G: Ipswich (printed material only)
23/9/H: Isle of Dogs
23/9/I: Kilburnie (printed material only)
23/9/J: Leatherhead
23/9/K: Leeds
23/9/K2: Leek
23/9/L: Leicester
23/9/M: Liverpool

23/9/N: London : general, including raids on City and Putney
23/9/O: London : fire watching
23/9/P: London areas: Fulham
23/9/Q: London areas: Hendon
23/9/R: London areas: Lewisham
23/9/S: London areas: Notting Hill Gate
23/9/T: London areas: Stepney
23/9/U: London areas: Streatham
23/9/V: Loughborough
23/9/W: Lowestoft

REEL 126

BOX 10 : AIR RAIDS IN BRITAIN, 1940-41 TOWNS M - Z
23/10/A: Manchester
23/10/B: Middlesbrough
23/10/C: Newcastle
23/10/D: Norwich
23/10/E: Northampton
23/10/F: Oxford
23/10/G: Petersfield
23/10/H: Plumstead
23/10/I: Plymouth
23/10/J: Portsmouth
23/10/K: Radlett
23/10/L: Redcar
23/10/M: Romford
23/10/N: Salford
23/10/O: Scunthorpe
23/10/P: Sheffield
23/10/Q: Southend
23/10/R: Southampton
23/10/S: Swansea
23/10/T: Swindon
23/10/T2: Trowbridge
23/10/U: Watford
23/10/V: West Bromwich
23/10/W: Wolverhampton
23/10/X: Woodbridge
23/10/Y: Worcester
23/10/Z: York and North Riding

REEL 127

TC 23, BOX 11: AIR RAIDS 1940-42

23/11/A: Survey on attitudes to compulsory ARP work, January 1941
Small number of interviews in London area on following questions :

- Should ARP work be made compulsory ?
- If yes, should this apply to both men and women ?
- Should the army help with ARP work ?
- Should fire watching be compulsory for private premises ?

Tabulations of results included

23/11/B: Fire-fighting, 1939-41
Selected leaflets and duplicated instructions
Observations on fire fighting activities in London
Diary extracts (Harrisson) September 1941; (Smallbones) January 1942

23/11/C: Gas masks, 1941-42
Counts of numbers of people carrying gas masks.
Report on a mock gas attack, Putney High Street, London
Description of poster on gas
For detailed information *see* GAS MASKS

23/11/D: Bombs in Hendon, February - March 1941
Account of bomb incidents by full-time Observer including accounts of interviews with local people

23/11/E: Air Raid Questionnaire, July 1941
Survey carried out in Oxford and London on people's expectations of further heavy raids
Report of results included

23/11/F: News Quota, March 1941
Report on the effect on the public of hearing that 9 German planes had been brought down

23/11/G Shelters, 1941
Counts of people using public shelters, London areas, March 1941.
Correspondence about sheltering and types of shelters

Survey on shelter preference: questions in the street about choice of shelter, brick or Anderson, February 1941
Survey results : questions on the Morrison (indoor) shelters
News cuttings on sheltering
People's views on the effects of fog on the likelihood of raids, February 1941

23/11/H Shelter Survey proposed by the *British Journal of Psychology* (Social Psychology Section), 1941
Comparison of plans for survey from Gertrude Wagner, Marie Jahoda and others. Critique by JF (M-O)
Report of discussion between psychologists

23/11/I: Chislehurst Caves, August 1941
Impressions and observations of people using the caves as air raid shelters. Includes survey on people's use of the caves

23/11/J: Fire Bomb Fritz Questionnaire, September 1941
Reactions to the new Ministry of Home Security advertisement on dealing with fire bombs

23/11/K: Warden's post, June 1941
Description of an ARP post, appearance, facilities, personnel, organisation, with an account of one evening's activities

23/11/L: Argument at a Warden's post, April 1941
Correspondence relating to a complaint against personnel at an ARP post in Twickenham

23/11/M: Home Guard, 1941
Report from a young member of the Home Guard (EG). Description of routines, incidents. May - June 1941

23/11/N: Police, 1941
Check by Mass-Observation to see how good were police directions for finding Citizens Advice Bureaux

23/11/O: "Blitz information", 1941
Article "Blitz information - the lifeline of Civil Defence" by Tom Harrisson **in** *Local Government Service,* August 1941
Criticism of availability of post-raid information
Replies and correspondence to criticism

REEL 127, TC 23, BOX 11 (continued)

Copies of local government information booklets

23/11/P: Wearing white in the blackout
Comparisons of counts 1940, 1941, and 1942

REEL 128

TC 23, BOX 12: AIR RAIDS 1942-45

23/12/A: Reprisals
Comparison of public attitudes towards bombing reprisals, 1940, 1941, and 1942

23/12/B: Civil Defence workers, 1942
Indirect comments, mainly from Hampstead, on Civil Defence Workers' attitudes to be released to take part time jobs, April 1942
Fire watching registration Kilburn, October 1942
Assorted duplicated papers on ARP education
Assorted papers on ARP education
Assorted notes on fire watching
Forms issued by the National Association of Girls' Training Corps, with correspondence

23/12/C: Air raid alert and sheltering, 1942
Indirect comments and observations of people' reactions to air raid alerts in various parts of London, 16.3.42
Observation in air raid shelters : Regent Square, St. Pancras and Museum Tube Shelter, 30.3.42

23/12/D: Air raids and sheltering, 1943
Indirect comments and observations

23/12/E: Air raids on London, June 1944
Reactions to the pilotless planes : indirect comments, observations and letters

23/12/F: Air raids on London, 1944
Assorted reactions to raids, overheard comments and observations, including account of Tube sheltering
Typed special report on unofficial noises, explosions and rumours about them. Sent in by volunteer, London, September 1944

23/12/G: Reaction to V2 bombs, 1945
Indirect comments with report

23/12/H: De-escalation of Civil Defence
Blackout: notes, 1943 and report on relaxation, 1944; lifting of blackout, 1945
Report on the stand down parade of part-timers in the National Fire Service, March 1945
Responses to special Directive on the lifting of the blackout, 1944, giving details of personal reactions and observations. Sent in by volunteers, September - October 1944
Press cutting from The *Yorkshire Post* on the lifting of the blackout, 18.9.44
Press cutting from The *Caterham Times* on the lifting of the blackout, 22.9.44

23/12/I: Diary extracts on air raids
Typed passages taken from war diaries sent to Mass-Observation, including a commentary

23/12/J: Tom Harrisson - air raid notes
Pencil notes (not very legible)

23/12/K: Mass-Observation volunteer Panel of Observers
Copy of letter from M-O to Observers asking for material, 20.11.40
Draft copy of Bulletin for Panel, 16.9.40, describing M-O's War Library

23/12/L: *Picture Post* article, 17.8.40
Notes, plans and draft mss for an issue of *Picture Post* on air raids; includes correspondence with Tom Hopkinson and poor photocopy of air raid article

23/12/M: Miscellaneous
Miscellaneous Notes, memos, letters etc. relating to Mass-Observation's study of air raids.

REEL 129

PROPAGANDA AND MORALE 1939-44

TC 43: 5 boxes

TC 43, BOX 1 : PUBLIC OPINION AND MORALE. 1939-42

43/1/A: Opinion Formation. December 1939-January 1940
Typed and handwritten interviews, (KB, JA, LE, HP, VMD, HN, JS, AFC, NM)
Extract:
"Mrs. Clarke, housekeeper, aged 62, Irish and brought up in Ireland, is widow with one daughter of 18, now sharing a flat with and looking after widower (Obs's farther). Not political. Voted Conservative at last election because told (by Obs's farther) she ought to. Otherwise would probably not have voted. Reads the Daily Express all through every day at odd "Five Minute" and takes it up to bed with her to finish off. Often reads an evening paper too. Does not read books except that she has been reading "The Mill on the Floss" for the last two years. She has reached page 36.

Asked how she forms her opinions about things of public interest: 'Just somehow you listen to what people say and read different papers, and somehow you form your own ideas about things, don't you.' "

43/1/B: Typed notes and reports on Public Opinion 1939-40
Note on M-O Opinion samples, 30.8.39
Memo "A Study of Opinion-Forming in a Limited Area" A Worktown Unit Bolton, 27.2.40 (AH)
Note "A Barometer of Public Opinion"
Notes "Institute of British Opinion", 1.5.40 (TH)
Report "What is Public Opinion?", 19.8.40 (M-O) (pp 4-5 missing)
Wartime Directive No. 3, and typed responses. November 1939

43/1/C: Miscellaneous-Morale. 1940-42
10 Analysis sheets estimating "pessimists" (related to type of job, income, area, age, etc.) Undated
3pp Statistics of overheards; January 40, March 41 (JF); March, April 41 (JA): "Subjects of conversation"
News clipping "Spring Attack by RAF" (February 42)
3 pp Handwritten notes on morale re postwar (August 42)

Typed, British Opinion Interviews, Preston 22.4.40 (AH), handwritten analysis
Handwritten replies to questions on Ministry of Information door to door canvass of public opinion, London 23.8.40
Typed impression of week's morale December 1940, Streatham (LE), Kilburn (CF), (GH)
Handwritten memo, good and bad morale signs, 3.4.41 (KT)
Handwritten notes on press reports on German outrages in occupied countries, 18.8.41
Handwritten revised Index of Morale, monthly averages, 1941-44
Typed appendix, "Home Morale and Public Opinion" , October 1941, Home Intelligence
Typed Interim Reports from the National Institute of Economic and Social Research
Handwritten lists of male and female prejudices
Weekly morale reports, June 41 (DH, JS, GD, NN, LF) Handwritten

43/1/D: Stimulus and Response (Date unknown)
Answers to a word association test. Male and female; undergraduates and adults

43/1/E: Draft article by TH (see File Report 2067) for "The Mood of Britain". 1944

REEL 130

TC 43, BOX 2 : PROPAGANDA THEORY 1939-44

43/2/A: Typed extracts re propaganda and the Ministry of Information. 1939
Typed press extracts, September/October (TH)
Pamphlet *The German News Agency and the News*, December 1939
Typed extracts from books

43/2/B: Correspondence (TH), 1939-41
Extract:
Tom Harrisson *"[Mass-Observation's] value is that it tells us exhaustively about the lower professional group (shopkeepers, clerks, civil servants) who probably dominate the country numerically and otherwise."*

REEL 130, TC 43, BOX 2 (continued)

43/2/C: Typed report on Morale/Propaganda 1940 (M-O)
Plus handwritten notes by Tom Hopkinson (see File Report 193)

43/2/D: Internal memos and notes 1939-41
Typed memo "Emergency Problems and Mass-Observation" August 1939
Typed article "The Public Needs Information" (TH)
Typed memo "The Five Channels of Publicity" (TH) October 1939
Typed memo sent to Mary Adams (TH) October 1939
Typed notes on propaganda
Typed observations at a meeting "Technique of Propaganda", 12.2.40 (LE)
Handwritten notes on propaganda techniques, August 1941 (JSF)
Typed notes "Some Maxims of Publicity"
Handwritten notes on 'The War of Jenkin's Ear' (16th century historical reference) (TH)

43/2/E: Ministry of Information 1938-41
Typed notes, observations, August-October 1939 (TH)
Handwritten notes (TH)
Typed, Ministry of Information "Plan for Home Publicity Policy" December 1940
Ministry of Information Bulletin "National Scheme for Propaganda by Window Display" August 1940
Typed copy "Themes for Propaganda" from Mary Adams 2.7.41
Ministry of Information leaflet publicising "The War Today" open air meeting, July 1941
Ministry of Information leaflet "British Empire Publicity Campaign", May 1941
Handwritten observations, Ministry of Information speaker, Hyde Park, June 1940 (CP)
Ministry of Information list of pamphlets 29.9.38
Press-cuttings
Copy of Ministry of Information Defence Notices, 1941
Prosecutions under Defence Regulations, typed details of selected cases, 29.7.40

43/2/F: Various reports and articles on propaganda (non M-O) 1939-44
Reports by:-BBC; Tom Wintringham; The War Office; Douglas Jay; Advertising Service Guild; Porter Sargent (USA); EM Wright; Tom Driberg; OJ Hale; Professor FC Bartlett; Office of the Lord Privy Seal; P Senft

Articles in:-*The New Statesman*, 2.9.39 "Propaganda or Information"; *Agenda*, August 1944 "The Problem of Propaganda"

REEL 131

TC 43, BOX 3 : BEAVERBROOK CAMPAIGNS 1940-42

43/3/A: Paper Salvage 1940
Typed observations, Worcester 20.9.40 (JA)
Typed report of first Anti-Waste meeting, 16.1.40 (JA), cutting from *The New Statesman* 30.12.39
Typed report of Traders Federation, 5.1.40 (JA)
Typed telephone interview with JA Poole, 8.1.40 (JA)
Typed report of Small Traders meeting, London, 18.1.40 (JA). 2 leaflets collected at the meeting

43/3/B: Paper Salvage October-November 1941
Typed and handwritten observations and overheards:-Hendon (JS); Notting Hill Gate (DH); Kilburn (CF); Kensington (JS); Willesden (PG); WC 1 (CM)

43/3/C: Paper Salvage 1942
Handwritten and typed copies of questionnaire
Replies to the questionnaire, (RCC, LB, PJ, EG)
Handwritten analysis of questionnaire (DB)
Analysis sheets and Handwritten indirects (LB, EG, PJ, MS)
Observations and counts of waste paper in rubbish bins, (LB, RCC, PN, EG, PJ)
Handwritten summary of direct observations (DB)
Observations in the Willesden area, 8.4.42 (LB)
Typed observations at Salvage Exhibition, Ford Showrooms 14.5.42 (CM)
Handwritten observations at "Waste Paper goes to War" exhibition, Selfridges, 27.5.42 (LB)
Typed observations "The World's Largest Waste Paper Basket" 31.1.42 (JS), Palmers Green

43/3/D: Bone Salvage June/July 1942
Typed questionnaire, 30.6.42
Handwritten and typed replies to questionnaire, June/July 1942, London (LB, CM, MS, EG)
Interview, examples of posters, handwritten (LB)
Analysis sheets

REEL 131, TC 43, BOX 3 (continued)

43/3/E: Leaflets and Press-cuttings 1940-41
Commercial cards asking for rags etc
Anti-waste leaflets produced by London Boroughs
Nation-wide leaflets produced by the Ministry of Supply
Press-cuttings

43/3/F: Rubber Salvage 1942
Typed report "Note on Rubber Salvage Campaign", 24.4.42

43/3/G: Aluminium Collection/Anti-waste Campaign
6 Observer reports on Aluminium 1940
4 Leaflets about Anti-waste Campaign

REEL 132

TC 43, BOX 4 : GOVERNMENT ADVERTISING CAMPAIGNS

43/4/A: Lightship leaflet April 1940
7 copies of the "Lightship leaflet"
Typed critique of the leaflet, Dr RA Macdonald
Handwritten and typed responses of the public to the leaflet, (CP, CF, NM, SS, HP, LE, BW, HN)
Handwritten analysis
Typed report "The Lightship Leaflet" (M-O)

43/4/B: The Silent Column July 1940
Typed supplementary report "The Silent Column and Government Advertising" 29.7.40 (M-O)
Interviews re advertisement, London, typed and handwritten
Typed analysis
Typed draft of test advertisement from newspapers (TH)
Analysis sheets and 2 press-cuttings

43/4/C: The New Magna Carta League Questionnaire October 1940
Re civil liberties, government advertising and the Ministry of Information
Typed manifesto of "The New Magna Carta League" John Tenney, November 1938
Typed and handwritten questionnaire responses (LE, DH, JS)
Analysis sheets

43/4/D: "The Greatest Crusade" Questionnaire October 1940
Typed and handwritten questionnaire responses, London (LE, JS, SS)
Press-cutting of the advert for "The Greatest Crusade"
Handwritten analysis (JSF)
Analysis sheets

43/4/E: Use Less Water Questionnaire, London 1941
Sketch of poster "Save Water"
Carbon of questionnaire
Typed and handwritten responses to questionnaire (MS, VT, DH, CF)
summary, general impressions and analysis (VT)
Analysis sheets

43/4/F: Blankets for Russia January 1942
Typed summary (EL)
General impressions (VW, EG, VT, RF, EL)
Notes (TH)
Analysis sheets

43/4/G: Blankets for Russia January 1942
Typed and handwritten responses to questionnaire (CM, BW, VT, VW, MC, EG), Kings Cross, Edgeware Road, Letchworth

43/4/H: Warships Week March 1942
Handwritten and typed observations in Portsmouth (MT), Leamington Spa (RCC) and London (LB, RCC, EG, PN)
Leaflets collected re Warships Week (LB, PN)
Copy of *The Evening News* Portsmouth and Southsea, 23.3.42
Typed Observations, Malmsbury (CF) 7.2.42

43/4/I: Miscellaneous
Copy prints of Government adverts
Handwritten list of Goverrunent advertising slogans

REEL 133

BOX 5 : MINISTRY OF INFORMATION EXHIBITIONS 1940-44

43/5/A: Typed reports and memos re exhibitions 1941
Typed memo from Mr Carter of RIBA, "Exhibitions, comments and questions", 7.10.41

REEL 133, TC 43, BOX 5 (continued)

Typed report "Government Exhibitions" (M-O) 1941
Handwritten memo from (JS), exhibitions, 27.8.41
Ministry of Information Exhibition Programme 1941-42

43/5/B: Morale Exhibitions 1940
Handwritten observations, indirects at Scrap exhibition Charing Cross, 21.8.40 (JS) and Typed observations Navy Exhibition, 27.10.40 (HP)
Handwritten observations "London Pride" Charing Cross, 18.12.40 (JF)
Typed observations, overheards, Messerschmitt on view, Croydon 23.8.40 (HP)

43/5/C: Ministry of Information photograph and poster exhibitions 1941
Handwritten summary of exhibitions, 3.9.41 (VT)
Typed summary of exhibitions, 8.8.41 (CF)
Reports, overheards and follows by full-time observers:
"Fighting the Fire Bomb": handwritten and typed, Worcester August (MS, DH, CF); handwritten, Twickenham August (MS, DH) and leaflet
"New Life to the Land": handwritten, Tottenham, 22.8.41 (JS)
"Free Europe's Forces": typed, Putney August/September (CF, PG) and leaflet
"Women at War": handwritten, East Finchley 29.8.41 (JS) and press-cutting; handwritten, Catford 29.8.41

43/5/D: Practical Exhibitions 1941
Summary of exhibitions, typed and handwritten, September (CF, VT)
Reports, overheards and follows by full-time observers:
Munitions exhibition: Worcester, August (CF, VT, DH); North Finchley, August (VT); Bolton (CF); leaflet and press-cutting
Food Advice Centre: Worcester, Hammersmith, August (VT, MS), leaflets
WVS Salvage exhibition: Putney, August (PG)
National Silage Campaign: Worcester, August (VT) , leaflets
Poison Gas exhibition: Shepherds Bush, Charing Cross, August/ September (MS, NN, DH)

43/5/E: Special Reports by members of the Panel, 1941
Handwritten and typed reports by the panel on Ministry of Information exhibitions in various areas

43/5/F: Propaganda exhibitions 1942-44
Fuel exhibition, typed observations, Charing Cross 23.9.42, (POL)
"Life-lines" handwritten observations, Catford 25.4.42 (EG)
"Paper Goes to War" exhibition. London, handwritten observations 25.1.43 (MS)
"Potato Pete's Fair", typed observations, London 1.1.43 (LB) and leaflets
"The 2 Mrs Britains" typed observations, London 1.9.43 (LB), and leaflet
"Colour in Everyday Life" typed observations, London 23.2.44, (LB)
"War in Wax" exhibition, typed observations, London 26.1.44, (LB) and leaflet
Daily Express War exhibition, typed observations, London, 3.7.44 (GST)

REEL 134

LONDON SURVEY 1940

TC 65: 5 boxes

Between July and October 1940, full-time Mass-Observers carried out a study of public behaviour and attitudes in London areas. The results of the study are divided up by weeks over a period of 14 weeks. The range of subjects studied is broad and although many themes are repeated, the subjects also vary from week to week. The main emphasis is on public morale in the weeks immediately before and during the first air raids on London. Observations were carried out in public houses, cinemas, churches, shops, on public transport, at rallies and meetings and in the street.

Overheard reactions to news reports on the radio were gathered; newspaper placard messages were recorded; shop window displays were noted for war references. Mass-Observation was particularly concerned with the effects of air raid warnings and air raids themselves on everyday life: sleeping arrangements, health, food, clothing, work, leisure, "nerves", children; attention was also given to safety provision (shelters) and to the effectiveness of public information (posters, films, leaflets, broadcasts by public figures such as Duff Cooper of the Ministry of Information). Rumours, grievances and "questions uppermost in the public mind" were recorded. Counts of people carrying gas masks gave an indication of whether people expected gas attacks.

A good deal of the study was carried out in Stepney and in Fulham but other London areas covered include Streatham, Notting Hill Gate, Kilburn, and the

REEL 134, TC 65, BOX 1 (continued)

West End. Mass-Observation personnel involved in this survey included: HP, CF, LE, NM, SS, DH, CP, JS.

The material has been kept together in individual weeks and is arranged in chronological order with reports by the same investigator grouped together. It is therefore possible to find, for example, a survey of attitudes to Gracie Fields divided between files because it was carried out by different investigators. The contents of this Topic Collection overlap with TC 23: Air Raids, TC 43: Propaganda and morale, TC 25: Political attitudes and TC 54: Police, law, and Invasion. Researchers are advised to check handlists to these Topic Collections for complementary material

TC 65, BOX 1: WEEK 1: UP TO AND INCLUDING WEEK ENDING 2.8.40

65/1/A:
News and morale; Molotov's speech; radio listening habits; political activity in Stepney: CPGB meeting; Dockers' meeting at Tower Hill; *Daily Worker* Gala and Fete; Activities in Fulham: cookery demonstrations; ARP unit of neighbours; interviews with Mayor; aliens in East End; Shelters: Anderson/other provision; allotments; ARP lecture; "Pots to Planes" Campaign; Regional Information Office Bulletins; street chalkings; newspaper placards; wayside pulpits; shop counts; effect of war on trade; ARP equipment (gas masks, ear plugs, stirrup pumps, torches and batteries); egg shortages; fashions; shop window displays

65/1/B:
Radio listening in pubs (news); newspaper placards; war references in *Picture Post* advertisements; church services; parties; Chamberlain; allotments in Fulham; Wandsworth Greyhound track; 'Rout the Rumour' Rally, Hendon Park; Royal Navy shop window display; Church Army women and prostitutes; shop windows; shopping observations; bulletin boards; church services; visitors to London landmarks, including Cenotaph

65/1/C:
'Rout the Rumour' Rally; clothing and fabrics; news reactions; Molotov's speech; newspaper hoardings; the 'Silent Column' and "Careless Talk" advertisements; aliens; ARP equipment; Portobello Market; Paddington Station; church serices; air raid rumours; War Artists Exhibition at National Gallery; advertising: war themes

REEL 135

BOX 2: LONDON WEEK 2: 3-9.8.40 ... WEEK 3: 10-16.8.40

London Week 2: 3-9.8.40
65/2/A:
Shelters in Stepney, use of gardens; air raid warnings; shortages and war effects on trade; political activity: Stepney Tenants Defence League and an interned resident; August Bank Holiday; "Stay Put" leaflet; street accident; newspaper hoardings; press campaign against Duff Cooper; clothes; air raids and nerves; church services

65/2/B:
Air raid in Thames Ditton; North Paddington Divisional Labour Party meeting; attitudes to news in general and to Duff Cooper; press posters

65/2/C:
Hammersmith Palais, dance; Coombe Hill Golf Club; attitudes to Duff Cooper; air raid shelter provision, Fulham; church service; children's playground; Gracie Fields; Hyde Park speech; internment of aliens and Jewish refugees; availability of goods; barrel organs

65/2/D:
Gracie Fields; cinema programme: Royal, Streatham; London Hippodrome Show; Duff Cooper; news reactions; WAAF exhibition at Selfridges

65/2/E:
Response to news; Gracie Fields, trade and hire purchase in wartime; air raid warning in Stepney; clothing; European Blockade; drawing unemployment benefit; the Vigilance Committee (redistribution of wealth in Romford); Ministry of Information meeting, Woodford; "Stay Where You Are" leaflet

London Week 3: 10-16.8.40
65/2/F:
Radio news reactions; Gracie Fields; European Blockade; air raid on Croydon Aerodrome; air raid alarm in Streatham; Holborn Empire (music hall); film trade; "Miss Grant Goes to the Door" (film about invasion); propaganda; MoI film: "Albert's Savings", "Just William" and various other films: reactions; Mrs Churchill and Duff Cooper at Woodford Rally; WVS and salvage

REEL 135, TC 65, BOX 2 (continued)

65/2/G:
West End air raids; unemployment; soldiers; military equipment in shop displays; women's fashions; European blockade; reports of air raids

65/2/H:
Air raid warnings; "Stay Where You Are" leaflet; Gracie Fields; Duff Cooper at Woodford; dinner dance at Cafe de Paris; Lords cricket match; Fulham tennis courts; newspaper placards; children in Fulham

65/2/I:
Letter-writing; Harrods Food Exhibition; Finchley toy shop displays; Gracie Fields; Labour exchanges; "Stay Where You Are" leaflets; blockade of Europe; Duff Cooper at Woodford; shop displays

REEL 136

BOX 3: LONDON WEEK 4: 17-23.8.40 ... WEEK 5, 24-30.8.40

London Week 4: 17-23.8.40
65/3/A:
Radio in factories; effect of war on shopkeepers; air raid warnings; Duff Cooper; reactions to news; newspaper placards; aerial activity over South London; meaning of word "Crusade"; political meetings; gas mask count

65/3/B:
Baptist Church service; air raids; Duff Cooper's broadcast; Messerschmitt 109 on display; interview with hairdresser on effects of war on trade; morale; grievances; Hyde Park Corner speakers; car accident; reactions to news; gramophone exhibition; scrap metal exhibition; household equipment

65/3/C:
Air raids; war talk in working men's cafe; air raid damage, Croydon; air raid casualties and funerals; audience response to films: "Sea Fort", "Let George Do It", Gaumont British News; evacuation of Somaliland; British Israel meeting; United Christian Witness meeting; music halls

65/3/D:
Overheards on air raids; Duff Cooper's broadcast; shortages of ARP

supplies; shortage of groceries; audience response to "Let George Do It,"; superstition; press posters; the word "Crusade"; pacifism; anti-alien feeling; invasion leaflet; women's organisations; funfairs and amusement arcades; posters in Notting Hill Gate Underground

London Week 5: 24-30.40
65/3/E:
Bus accidents; jazz music; "Internment of Aliens" leaflet; air raids and sleep; people in pubs listening to news; the sound of the air raid siren; Duff Cooper and the MoI Social Survey; unexploded bomb, Chelsea

65/3/F:
Air raids and warnings; the morning after; health and nerves; Paddington Station crowds; sound of siren; Spitfire Fund; Home Guard; soldiers; pacifists; internment of aliens; Portobello Market; press posters; war toys; Women's Guild of Empire

65/3/G:
Work in wartime; WAAF; sleep during raids; social life and air raids; behaviour during warnings; personal and domestic life; pacifists; RAF achievements

65/3/H:
Air raids and warnings; internment of aliens; children; Stepney schools; children's concert at National Gallery; Mutual Aid of Good Neighbours Association; press coverage of the war; political meetings; shelters

REEL 137

TC 65, BOX 4: WEEK 6: 31.8.40-6.9.40, WEEK 7: 7-13.9.40

Week 6: 31.8.40-6.9.40
65/4/A:
Air raid at Radlett, Herts; Fulham street observations; air raid warning, Streatham; reactions to news; internment of aliens; Duff Cooper on "Children's Hour"; British Paramount News and MoI film and air raid interruptions in Brixton; air raid shelters; newspaper posters in West End; Spitfire Funds; Holloway Labour Exchange; smoking habits; clothes wearing; grievances and rumours; Hampstead Hurricane Fund
Extract:
"This village of Radlett is not more than twenty miles from London. But the

REEL 137, TC 65, BOX 4 (continued)

impression that many people have is that London is razed to the ground, 'crucified' as a waiter said. One lady living in St John's won't risk even going back for a day to her house , another refuses to visit her house in Kensington. Apparently part of this scare has been caused by a lady from Golder's Green who had produced some very vivid stories."
Radlett, 2/9/40

65/4/B:
Air raid, Belgravia; Internee leaflet; Spanish war posters exhibition; Conscientious Objectors Tribunal; nerves in air raids; Duff Cooper's "Come on Hitler" broadcast; church service and air raid warning; rumours and jokes; Hyde Park; Cycling Club, Slough; classical music; air raids; ARP counter at Woolworths; bedding arrangements in air raids; gas mask counts

65/4/C:
Alma Wittlin of United Correspondents; air raids; theatre: "Chu Chin Chow", bomb incident, Stepney Green Station; conscientious objectors; Portobello Market; Victoria Bus Terminus; ARP; press posters; jobs; fashions in Oxford Street; gas masks; smoking habits; rumours

65/4/D:
Aerial activity over Stepney; air raids in Stepney: arrangements, shelters, sleeping arrangements, gas mask wearing; General de Gaulle; the services call up, registration pay, Dunkirk, attitudes to officers

Week 7: 7-13.9.940
65/4/E:
Air raid; East End evacuation; Isle of Dogs; reactions to news; sleeping and air raids; bomb damage at Buckingham Palace; the weather; grievances and rumours; anti-semitism in Poplar; graffiti; air raid victim's funeral, Stepney; morale in shelters; restaurants and shops in air raids; work; ARP in Kilburn; press posters; lack of safety in shelters; Spanish soldiers and Norway invasion

REEL 138

TC 65, BOX 5: WEEK 8: 14-20.9.40, WEEK 9: 21-27.9.40, WEEK 10: 28.9.40-3.10.40, WEEK 11: 4-10.10.40, WEEK 12: 11-17.10.40, (WEEK 13): missing, WEEK 14: 25-31.10.40

65/5/A: Week 8: 14-20.9.40
Air raids; evacuation; morale; invasion; sleep during raids; attendance at church, places of entertainment and libraries in central London; newspaper articles; leisure activities; brick shelters; Thames Water Buses Emergency Service; National Arbitration Tribunal Panel (Bank Officers Guild v. Barclay's Bank), observations in billiards room and social club

65/5/B: Week 9: 21-27.9.40
East End evacuees; air raid shelters in Underground Stations; shelters and safety; pub count; Chamberlain; internment; observation in parish church; feelings about air raids and death; Brynston Floor 'nippies' on leisure, Lord Haw Haw and air raids and work; schools as rest centres; children's behaviour; Tilbury Docks Shelter; homes damaged by bombs

65/5/C: Week 10: 28.9.40-3.10.40
Air raids; seeking security; evacuation and refugees; sleep in raids; shops damaged by raids; shelters; Southwark Shelter; pubs on routes out of London; posters; household readjustments and special arrangements in air raids

65/5/D: Week 11: 4-10.10.40
Tube shelters; graffiti in telephone kiosks; sleep; 'Bomb Berlin' poster; reception of refugees from London in Windsor; Rest Centre and evacuation office; government press advertising; homelessness; anti-semitism; Rest Centre in London; organisation of ARP wardens; patrolling during blitz; non-evacuated mothers and children; residents/evacuees relations

65/5/E: Week 12: 11-17.10.40
Evacuation; soldiers; effect of weather on air raids; General de Gaulle; Princess Elizabeth's speech; Ministry of Information; plans for after the war: savings, time-keeping, sex life, attitudes to government; estate agents on rent decreases and evacuation

(Week 13: missing)
65/5/F: Week 14: 25-31.10.40
Lyons Teashop in air raid; communal basement in Kilburn during raid

Crisis (Conversations) 3 ja 1.9.39

3 The George, Strand.

Obs asked young man of about 25, office worker, dressed in black, for a light.

Obs "Do you think they'll declare war toninght ?"

M "They'll give Hitler a 12 hour ultimatum, I expect -- they did in the last war".

Obs "Don't you think he'll strike as soon as possible ?"

M "Yes, I expect he will. I live right in the West End. But the bombing's sure to be pretty haphazard. They'll aim chiefly at breaking our morale, and at trying to hit our ammunition dumps. But they won't know where they are -- the average man in this country doesn't. I played cricket against the RAF at Uxbridge last week. They've all moved into "hidey holes", as tiy call them. You just imagine an untrained pilot -- after all, none of these fellows have had any experience -- he won't hit his objective. The bombs will be scattered all over the place, and any he's got left over will be dropped on the South coast resorts. Anyway, think of a modern machine gun in a trench -- if a plane comes over, what chance will it have ? Those guns can pump hundreds of bullets in a second -- they'd tear a plane to bits.

Hitler says he's only bombing military stations, and the Poles admit that it's true. You can't believe the newspapers -- they print a pack of lies.

Crisis Conversations (TC 23, Box 1/B, p3)

Crisis (Conversations) 4 ja 1.9.39

Of course women and children have been hit -- there are bound to be women and children in any town. And I think Russia will support them,and so will Italy. This statement issued tonight doesn't mean a thing. The war will be a case of the French walking through the Siegfried line to Berlin. I know the Siegfried line is supposed to be impregnable but it was built in a much greater hurry than the Maginot line. The Maginot line is an underground town,with special trains running to carry spare rifles. The Siegfried line is nothing like so strong.

This situation is getting on people's nerves -- you can notice it all around you. We've got some fellows in our office -- they were officers in the last war. They came out nervous wrecks,and now they've been given cushy jobs. I often do the jobs of fellows getting 3 or 4 times my salary -- they're the most inefficient fellows in the office. You can tell what effect the strain is having. There are some nasty buggers in our office -- they've turned quite nice now. The there are one or two girls I can't get on with -- but they're willing to do anything for you at the moment."

(Enter middle-aged man in Air Force uniform. He orders a drink at the bar.)

Barmaid "You changed quickly -- quicker then Hitler,the old bastard. Who did it for you ?"

Crisis Conversations (TC 23, Box 1/B, p4)

Crisis (Conversations) 5 ja 1.9.39

RAF "Rome wasn't built in a day"

Bar "No, but it could be blown up in half an hour".

M (to obs) "I'd like to ask this bloke about a short term commission. They're for 5 years, but I don't want to be landed in anything. You get some rotten fellows in some of the services. I saw some Terriers the other day -- they were a nasty lot, the lowest you could imagine. Then there's more snobbery in the Air Force than in any other service. I know a fellow who in a surveyor's office and he was chucked out for getting drunk. First of all the boss caught him in a pub during hours, then he saw him drunk one night -- well, he said he was drunk, though I suppose he was just merry. He was married, too. He got a job in the RAF, but he couldn't get a commission -- I don't know why. Anyway, he was in the team that played against us at Uxbridge. We had tea in the officers mess, but they told him to get his in the kitchen -- wouldn't let him come with us.

After the match was over, we had a beer match -- each side batted for an hour, and the side that got most runs was given beer by the other side for the rest of the evening. Well, we lost, and it cost us 15/- each. They had a Wing Commander playing for them. At first, everyone was calling him "sir", but it ended up with you "old bugger, you old bastard".

(A fellow of about 30 comes to the bar and orders drinks. He is so hot he has taken his coat off. He

Crisis Conversations (TC 23, Box 1/B, p5)

AIR RAID WARNING.

-----oOo------

6/6/40
K Pards...

I was travelling up to Scotland from Kings Cross to Edinburgh by train on the night of Thursday June the 6th, (to write like a police court proceeding) - I was not in a Sleeping Car ~~by-a~~ but I was sharing a First Class carrige with a Naval Officer who had recently come on leave from Narvik, and was now returning to work. The carriage was extremely hot as it had been standing in a siding all day, and was now blacked out and blinded. Lights were still on in the carriages adjoining ours, but at 11 o'clock we turned ours out and went to sleep.

How long I slept I do not know (to quote from the detective stories) - somewhere which I quessed to be around 12.30 - I was woken up by the guard of the train who was coming down the corridor announcing to passengers

> 'There is an Air-Raid Warning. Passengers who want to, can get out at the next station, but the train is proceeding."

His announcement seemed to have very little effect on anyone in the adjoining carriages. There was so far as I could hear [redacted], little movement or noisy conversation. The Naval Officer in my carriage bestirred himself sufficiency to say "Thank you very much." ; I was unable to wake myself up sufficiently to do that.

As most of the passengers in the adjoining carriages were soldiers and sailors, many of whom must have come from such places as Dunkirk or Narvik, the announcement could hardly be expected to create a great reaction. As for myself I felt [redacted] regrettably little interest, perhaps this was due to the fact that I was sleepy. I have never heard an Air-Raid Warning, and I heard no sirens now. I rather gather that the warning was given to the train by some system of signals (possibly but improbably radio) I made a decision that if I heard gun fire* I would go to the carriage window at the end of the corridor, which I believe was open, and see if there were any search lights. (*Distant gunfire)

Air-Raid Warning (TC 23, Box 5/A, p1)

(This would have been quite practic[redacted]able as there were no lights burning in the carriages.) I do not know whether this was because they had been switched out [redacted] by various individuals when they went to sleep, or a[redacted]together from main switch.

I heard no aeroplane engines and no gun-fire, and a few minutes later the all-clear was given, by the guard who returned.

Later in the night I was again woken up (almost) by the guard who announced another air-raid alarm. I cannot remember hearing him give the all-clear, and assume that I must have gone straight asleep again. In the morning I asked the Naval Officer what he thought a train would do in the event of an Air-raid: would it go straight on and be a train, or would it stand still and pretend it was only an Armament works. He said he thought it would get into a tunnel if there was one and hide. This conjured up the spectacle of what would happen in the tunnel if all the trains in the neighbourhood had the same idea.

What the train actually did do is obscure. The guard announced that it was proceeding, but it did so very slowly, and stopped repeatedly during the period of the alarm. It failed to make its connection at Edinburgh next morning. I do not know if it did any waiting in tunnels. My naval officer was possibly over-tunnel concious due to his experiences in Narvik. There are, I understand, sixty tunnels between Narvik and the Swedish Border. So far the Germans have been driven out of 19. That leaves forty one great British Victories still to come.

Air-Raid Warning (TC 23, Box 5/A, p2)

THE DAILY MIRROR, JUNE 20, 1940

12 KILLED IN FIRST BIG RAID

ONE hundred German bombers, attacking in waves, opened Germany's total air war on Britain early yesterday. Twelve civilians, five of them children, were killed and thirty others injured, but no military objectives were hit.

It was Germany's most ambitious raid yet. For attackers and defenders it was a night in a hundred.

R.A.F. fighters soared swiftly into the brilliant sky, striking mercilessly at the enemy. A.A. guns spat ceaselessly. So hot was their stream of fire that forty enemy bombers attacking at one point failed to penetrate inland and turned back.

Seven bombers were shot down, by the R.A.F. Enemy airmen were captured after their planes crashed.

Dawn was breaking in many of the towns on the East Coast of England when sirens shrilled the All-clear and people left their Anderson shelters. Some warnings lasted for four hours.

Alarms were given in Norfolk, Suffolk, Lincolnshire, Northamptonshire, Cambridgeshire, Yorkshire, Essex and the Thames Estuary.

This is how the various sections of the public reacted to the ordeal of the first mass attack.

Children who were not evacuated from towns raided on the Thames Estuary behaved magnificently.

They kept up the spirits of their parents and elders, and were not scared of bombs, planes, searchlights or sirens.

The Anderson shelters stood up well and though a few were penetrated by splinters from heavy bombs bursting at close range, the majority were undamaged.

In those shelters which had been hit the occupants of the houses had had no time to get to them, and stayed behind in a lower room of their homes.

✦ ✦ ✦

A.R.P. and first-aid men did grand work.

But they all complained that they had no time to organise themselves properly because the sirens here were not sounded until after the bombs had fallen.

Hospital Calm

The raid on one town provided the first real test for a British hospital under air raid conditions.

The result was described by the secretary as "very satisfactory."

For over an hour the whistle of bombs screaming through the air, and the crash of repeated detonations mingling with the roar of aircraft and the thud of A.A. fire was clearly heard.

"Without one solitary exception everybody behaved magnificently," said the secretary.

"The patients themselves—they were all ... remained calm and quiet."

He Never Whimpered

One story typical of many acts of courage comes from a house where an A.R.P. warden, Mr. Maurice Reginald Baker, lives with his wife and five-year-old son Nigel.

"Before I was out on the job," Mr. Baker said, "the first bomb, exploding in an adjoining garden, threw me down as I was bustling Nigel and my wife to safety in the house.

"I then went off to Frederick Jolley—the Mayor's chauffeur—but he had been killed by a bomb-splinter, and I spent the next half-hour attending to other cases.

"Then my wife, Nigel and my wife's sister went into our Anderson shelter with a neighbour's dog. The neighbours were the Cooks. They were all hit and went to hospital.

"All through the warning Nigel was peeping out and looking at the searchlights, shouting: 'Are they getting anywhere near him?' We did not hear a whimper out of him all the time."

Killed at His Door

One victim of the raids was killed because he was curious.

Harry Wisden, thirty-four, heard the bombardment begin in an Essex town, went to the front door, and was killed by a bomb splinter.

✦ ✦ ✦

Many people had narrow escapes, but were still able to laugh.

A Suffolk rector and his family were awakened by bombs which fell on either side of the rectory. They escaped unhurt.

The rector's wife said: "The bombs swept my chimneys for me free."

✦ ✦ ✦

By seeking refuge in shelters quickly many avoided serious injury.

Thirty-seven evacuated girls in a hostel in East Anglia went into a refuge when the siren went.

A bomber crashed into a large tree in the garden and burst into flames.

The matron declared that had the machine not hit the tree it would have struck the hostel.

✦ ✦ ✦

Noise of the raids, though intense, was not so bad as was expected.

One man in the centre of a district where many bombs fell said:

"The noise was terrific and at first frightening. But most people soon got used to it."

Nor was the damage as great as was feared.

Many bombs fell in one district of the Eastern Counties. The only casualty was a lorry driver standing beside his lorry. He received a slight wound.

Caravan dwellers only 150 yards away were unhurt and their caravans untouched.

✦ ✦ ✦

The public must not expect the R.A.F. to be always as successful as in this first big raid.

On nights when weather conditions are much less favourable, their task will be much harder.

As the number of hours of darkness increases, it will be increasingly difficult both for the raiders and for our fighters in going up to attack them.

German objectives in the East Coast raid ... bases; but this is what they bombed. . . .

In a Cambridgeshire town men clear ... in a street. The enemy didn't have it all on the preceding page.

At least seven crashed down—the rest ...

Rescue workers were kept busy after Britain's biggest raid. This Salvationist has brought out the washing from one of a row of houses which were hit by a bomb.

The Dead

The official list of those killed in the raid in Cambridgeshire is:—

Heather Dear, aged five months; Mr. William Langley; Mr. Sam Langley; Gladys Clarke, aged eleven; Mr. and Mrs. J. Beresford and their son Michael, aged two years; Molly Palmer, aged nine; and Leonard Palmer, aged six.

At the Thames Estuary town: Mr. Frederick Jolley; Mrs. Jane Edith Wallman; Mr. Harold Wisden, who had a leg amputated in hospital.

✦ ✦ ✦

In addition to these official casualties, two deaths are reported from heart failure—Mr. Edward James Milner, aged sixty-five, of Kent, and Mr. Harry Whitehead, aged sixty-nine, of Yorkshire.

...OT SHOT ... RAIDERS

... pilot patrolling over the ... down two of the seven ... in the first big raid on ...

... before 1 a.m. he saw a ...engined enemy bomber ... by a searchlight.

...ding rapidly, he attacked. ...d by his machine-gun bul... the bomber crashed in ... in Essex.

... the pilot, a flight-lieu... saw one of the German crew ... parachute.

... minutes later the same pilot ... German bomber held by ... beam over the Thames ... black crosses clearly in ...

... he climbed, engaged the ... and again the bomber ... in Essex.

...ed in Beams

... shot down a Heinkel ... Norfolk. Further south a ... was having a fight ... Heinkel as they dodged in and ... searchlight beams over the ...

... gunner hit the enemy ... bursts of bullets and put his ... out of action.

... R.A.F. fighters attacked ... bomber caught by search... Kent. Trying to escape, ... some thirty ... before it was shot down ...

Opposite you've seen damage done by the raiders. These pictures show the other side—four of the seven raiders brought down. And forty raiders couldn't pass the barrage at the coast . . turned back. The raider above crashed in a garden.

The R.A.F. got the better of the argument with this raider. It crashed in Cambridgeshire.

... LAST BOMB

Shot down by Spitfires during the east coast raid this Heinkel ended its career of destruction in the sea.

12 killed in First Big Raid (TC 23, Box 7/A)

EVENING STANDARD, June 19, 1940

LATE NIGHT FINAL

Evening Standard

Amusements 8
Radio 8

BLACK-OUT 9.48 pm, 4.15 am
MOON Rises 8.37 pm, Sets 5.31 am

No. 36,127 LONDON, WEDNESDAY, JUNE 19, 1940 ONE PENNY

7 GERMANS SHOT DOWN IN RAID BY 100 PLANES

The tail of one of the raiders brought down in East Anglia.

12 People Killed and 14 Injured

ROW OF HOUSES HIT

Seven German airplanes were shot down, in bombing raids lasting nearly four hours early to-day over the Thames Estuary and Eastern England.

TWELVE CIVILIANS ARE KNOWN TO HAVE BEEN KILLED AND FOURTEEN INJURED. NINE OF THOSE KILLED AND MOST OF THE INJURED WERE IN CAMBRIDGESHIRE WHERE A BOMB SHATTERED A TERRACE OF EIGHT HOUSES.

It is learned authoritatively in London that about 100 German airplanes took part in the raid.

R.A.F. fighters got five of the seven raiders which were brought down and almost certainly a sixth. The seventh was probably brought down by anti-aircraft fire.

It is believed that the enemy's main objective was the airfields on the East Coast. The damage generally was very slight, although bombs were dropped up and down the country.

One of the raiders crashed in Essex, another on the Norfolk Coast, a third in the sea off the East Coast,

7 Germans Shot Down (TC 23, Box 7/A)

From AASTA Rec 11/10/40

(3)

4t

ASSOCIATION OF ARCHITECTS SURVEYORS AND TECHNICAL ASSISTANTS

+ 21.2 (HOUSING COMMITTEE)

REPORT ON RE-HOUSING THE HOMELESS AND EVACUATION

The last four weeks of intensive bombing in London has raised most acute problems of air-raid protection, evacuation and re-housing. Members of the Housing Committee of the Association have carried out investigations in the worst of the bombed areas, mainly the riverside boroughs, and the proposals made in this memorandum are based on first-hand information.

THE PRESENT PROBLEM

It is the opinion of the Committees that there is as yet no sign of a bold policy, which alone can ease the present position.

There are now three main problems. The first to house the homeless, the second to arrange the evacuation of whose who wish to go to safer areas, and the third to make life possible for those who wish to, or must, remain in the danger areas. Here we deal in detail with the first two only, although the provision of bomb-proof shelters, communal feeding arrangements and the retention of the social and administrative structure of the danger areas are integral parts of a successful solution.

The people have lost faith in the blast and splinter proof protection which the Government provides and many are travelling far afield in a frantic search for safety. Evacuation of women and children is also passing out of the control of the authorities; people are now leaving London as refugees, not as evacuees under an organised scheme. The plight of the homeless is even more serious. They spend their nights in crowded and unprotected rest centres and their days rescuing what little remains of their shattered homes. In many cases the time taken in finding billets for them has been so long that despair and fear of being bombed again has driven them to the tubes. All this is happening when the casualties and destruction have by no means assumed the scale anticipated by the Government, according to statements in Parliament, for which, therefore, they should have made the necessary preparations.

The present chaos is the result of the accumulation of failures on the Government's part to carry out well planned schemes before extreme emergency arose. The Evacuation and A.R.P. Committees of the Association have, during the last two years, submitted proposals based on detailed research for bomb-proof

(p.t.o.)

3681

Association of Architects ... Report on Re-Housing (TC 23, Box 7/A)

(64) The War and the Farmer. Miss C. Jackson
TAC. 11. Bishop Auckland
12/12/40

We hear much of those unfortunate townspeople whose lives have been wrecked by enemy action. Bereaved and bewildered, penniless and homeless they indeed deserve sympathy and help.

But we are apt to forget that the well-being of many country people is also menaced. No sudden disaster for us – but we can see ruin rolling towards us. Slowly but inevitably!

First look at the plight of the general farmer. The feeding stuff he has ordered fails to arrive. Weeks pass only the common (poorer) foods are left. No cow-cake – so the milk yield decreases. Those in

The War and the Farmer (TC 23, Box 8/E)

Air Raid Report.

30/1

Nazi planes raided this district on Thursday. Clouds made an excellent screen for the raiders.

The nearest bomb dropped about four miles from here.

Two persons were killed – an evacuee boy and a deaf labourer. Ten cows and two horses were also killed.

Incendiary bombs caused a number of fires which were extinguished with remarkable speed.

Morale:—

Motorist: "I can't see how we will manage to beat them. They have so many planes."

Man, excitedly: "We can look out for it now. They will be over this weekend (14th). They can

- 1 -

Air-Raid Report (TC 23, Box 8/E, p1)

make planes faster than we can bring them down."

Newsagent: "Exciting, wasn't it?

Man (who was showing fragments of bombs): 'Silly, isn't it? .. Because he (Hitler) is done, finished any time!

Local shop assistant (girl): "Not many people talk about the raid" (i.e. conversation on Saturday)

Myself: No one seems interested in it."

Shop assistant, "That is just how I feel! If a bomb dropped quite near, say a few yards away – I would be frightened then. But until then I'm not bothered."

I heard comparatively few remarks about the raid. People were laughing and talking cheerfully about their own interests.

Personal comment: 'Thrilling!'

2

Air-Raid Report (TC 23, Box 8/E, p2)

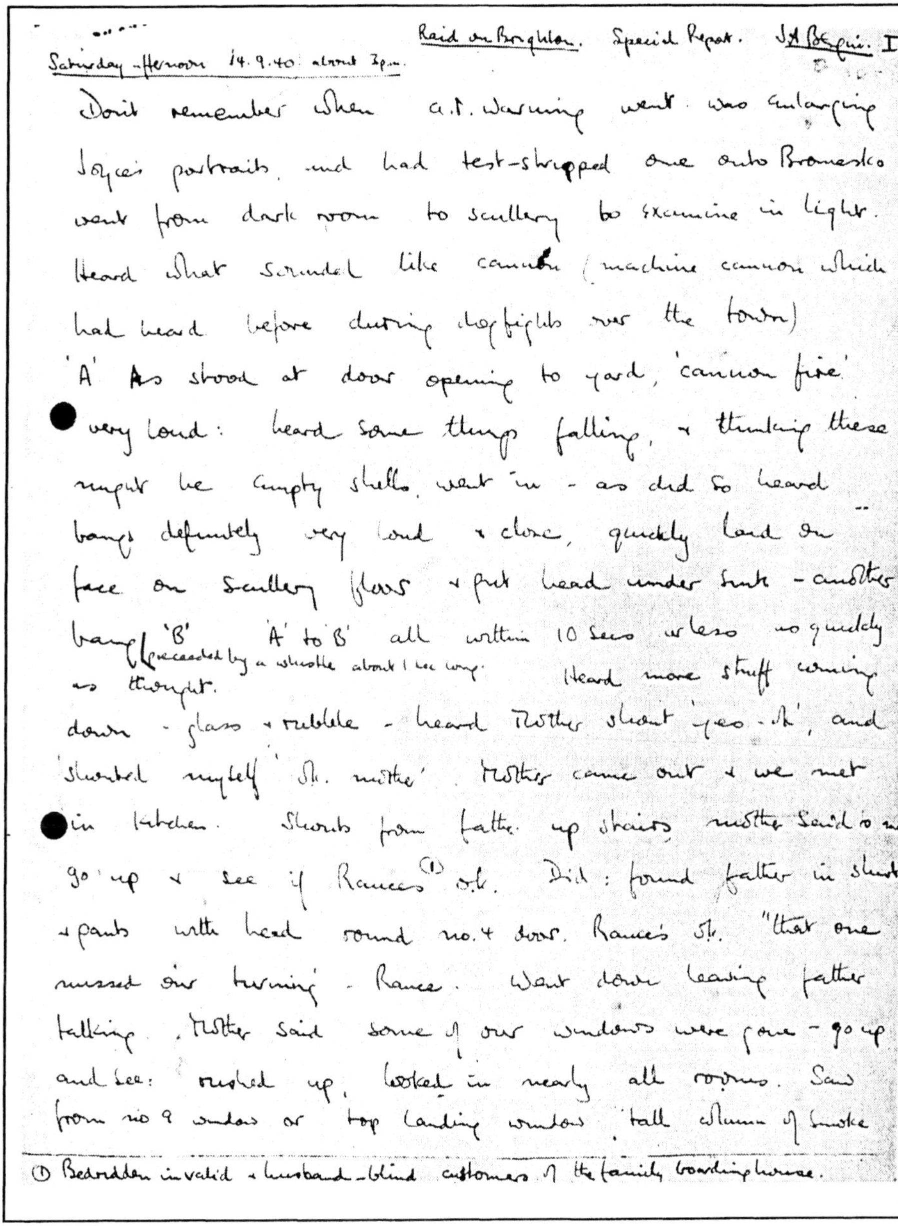

Raid on Brighton (TC 23, Box 8/H, p1)

room, from middle of Lloyds bank in St. Georges Terrace direction. Rushed down very fast, planes audible when got to basement. Mother & Mrs France (2) on hall floor, advised them to go down & they did to basement, found camera & exposure calculator, argued a bit with Mother about going out, Father down in basement by then. Went out into area & up steps, saw people on their steps, came back (may have heard a plane): in area found a bomb fragment still too hot to hold — which, shown to Mrs. France & Mother retained its heat a long while, Mrs F. showing it down very quickly — wandered into area & up steps and up slowly to St James's Street, where on the corner glass from 2nd hand furniture shop in the road. Walked towards the direction of the smoke, ie along St James's St. a few smashed shop windows along it. at bottom of Bedford St saw wreckage across the road & walked towards it. Appeared to be a direct hit on Chapman's baker's shop: thought poor old Chapman: A.R.P. & Police & other people running about. Two men covered with blood, sitting on left hand pavement groaning — being attended to by unskilled friends. Argument over getting an ambulance or taking them to F.A. Post. People running into remains of shop, went over to try to help. Didn't know how to start, & there were plenty there, saw bloke, about 19

(2) a neighbour

Raid on Brighton (TC 23, Box 8/H, p2)

II

I knew by sight for 15 years, crying etc. Supposed his people hit: felt no sympathy but only wanted him to shut up. Saw ambulance coming, wandered further up, looked along Hereford St, another bomb there: thought of Joyce(3), & walked up to Coalbrook Road & looked: all OK. in her terrace: went back, warden stopped me going down Bedford St. again; went along Eastern Road, where many broken windows, and down Lavender St. Houses in Hereford St damaged: heard warden ask thro' broken window, all OK in there, woman's voice, young lady injured not serious & he went on further. Wandered round again looking at damage, Lavender St, Essex St along to Bedford Street wreck, into Bedford St wounded gone, blood about on pavements – & on walls. Hung about a bit, then saw Walter & father & went off to Hospital.(4)

Didn't know where to start, got my tin hat & gas mask to look OK. and show I knew something of what was wanted. Somehow got on to shifting a corpse (old woman) on a door, very heavy (c.r.d.) with 3 other people, taking it out of front and post (S. side of Eastern Road) round to back of Hospital (N. Side) towards the garage where nurse (or sister) had said, on the way met 'Eddie' young porter who said later that he was 'in charge' of the mortuary. He said 'fill up the mortuary

(4) I then had a job overnight as night stretcher bearer – auxiliary fireman at the Hospital.
(3) The current girl friend.

Raid on Brighton (TC 23, Box 8/H, p3)

5/C

War Work Week. Finchley. 29-8-41

M.S.

Posters and Advertisements.

The exhibitions are well advertised by poster displays, advertisements in the local papers and by loud-speaker vans touring the streets announcing the times and places of the film shows and the exhibitions. These loudspeaker vans also make appeals for volunteers for women's war work - mostly patriotic in tone, though the inducement is put forward that training acquired now will be useful for an after-the-war career.

There are several large posters (about 7' 6" x 5') on hoardings in, or just off the main streets; and smaller ones (about 30" x 20") which also appear in shop windows, depicting a woman in a munitions overall carrying a banner - - - - - - -
(overall - brown, Banner, white lettering on black)
lettering brown, poster white)

Another fairly prevalent poster is in the smaller size (20" x 30") and advertises the film exhibitions and the M.O.I. poster display entitled "Women at War."

This one depicts a group of marching women headed by a brown-overalled munitions worker carrying a shell in her arms. Just behind are the uniformed services led by a WAAF on the lefthand side and an ATS on the right.

War Work Week (TC 43, Box 5/C)

Stepney. 9.8.40.

NM 9.p.m.

The Nine O'Clock News .

The basement of small house. Wireless is an old Marconi,- can only got about four stations . It is in the corner of the front room. Front room is in darkness - blackout is a long job, and seldom bothered with . Couch, table, chairs, etc. The back room is electrically lighted - ~~kitch~~ it s a sort of kitchen, with scrubbed table, gas-stove, sink, etc.

at 8.55p.m., M35C hurries in, and asks the time.

NM: Five to.

Man: I'll switch it on now - it may be slow. We don't want to miss the news.

Does so, and lays on couch, in darkness.
F35C (his wife) comes in silently, and sits on chair in kitchen.
M6 C (His mother) stumps down the stairs, and settles in a chair by the stove.

Wife goes to the kitchen blackout.

First announcement "This is the nine o'clock news . . ."

	"Here we are" (Man).
Summary. of news items	No response.
Communique about enemy attacks. . . .	
Mention of E-boats	Wife - "I've never heard of them. I know there were U-boats."
Losses of the enemy	"There you are" (Man)
"Raids by RAF" communique	
"All returned safely"	"Ha!" (Mother).
Fires destroy German petrol supplies.	N.R.
German attacks on this country	"I knew there was something going on all day." (Man.)
Leaflets.	"Ridiculous." (Man).
Casualties for July	N.R.
Comparison with road deaths . . .	"Dreadful - on the road!"(wife.)
Italians havn't advanced	Mother grunts, and goes upstairs.
Activity in Middle East	Man sighs from his couch.
Loss of HMS Oswald ".	"That s a good one in the paper. What does HMS stand for?"(Man) Wife motions him to be quiet. Man: "Hitler, Mussolini and Stalin. Pretty good, eh?" (Wife: Shhh!)
Indias statement.	"It s time they . " (Man). "I'm going to get my knitting."(wife) Wife goes out.
Security executive.	No response.
Skilled workers.	" "
	Man is listening intently.

The Nine O'clock News (TC 65, Box 2/A)

(5)

H.P.

14 JAN 1942

C.O. Tribunal

Fulham Town Hall, Jan 6th 1942.

There were some twenty of us conscientious objectors. We were dealt with ~~at~~ in alphabetical order which put me about number 15 on the list.

We sat on chairs in a semi circle round the walls – on a level with the judges. To have his case tried the individual descended into the well of the court room and stood beneath the judges.

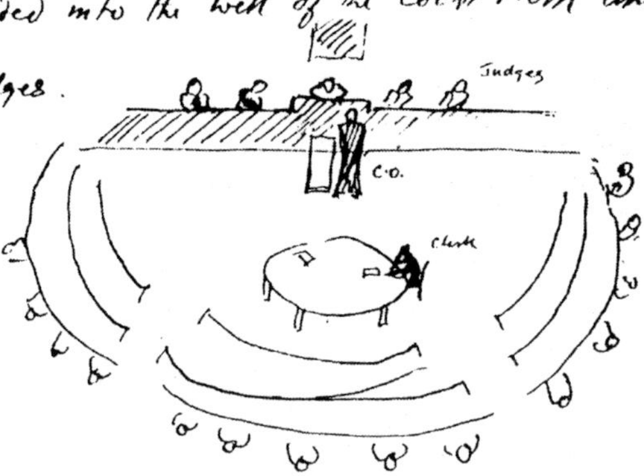

The procedure. The presiding judge read out the statement you had previously written to the tribunal. He then usually asked if you had anything you wished to add to it. He and (or) the other judges then asked questions. at some point you were asked for

C.O. Tribunal (TC 6, Box 1/B)

1.

1. Jean Henderson Salvation Army Clerk	The Judge reads out the statement. Judge: What have you done to acquaint yourself with the Christian attitude to this war? App: In my understanding of Christianity I cannot take part in this war. I feel that I am better employed as I am. The applicant then described how most of her free time was employed with social work connected with the Salvation Army. Judge asked if the App. had any letters. Two letters and a second statement were handed to the Judge. She said that she had no witnesses. App. was then asked to take a seat at the side of the court whilst the Tribunal made its decision.	Direct that she be registered as a C.O. to Combatant and Non Combatant duties and that she carry on with her present job.
2. Phyliss Beadell Counter Assistant at Woolwoths.	Judge reads out statement which said that App. had joined the Jehovahs Witnesses at the end of 1940. The statement included three quotations from the Bible. Dr Pickard, with Bible open on bench in front of him: Who was the speaker in that first quotation? App. I dont know Dr P: What is the chapter about? No answer. Miss Strudwick: Christ said "I come not with peace but with a sword. Do you remember that?" No answer. The applicant was then asked whether she had attended any places of worship before joining the Jehovahs Witnesses. App. said she had not. The App's mother gave witness to her daughter's sincerity.	Direct that her name be removed from the register of C.Os
3. Mary Sarah Frost Draper's assistent.	Judge read statement in which App. said that her objection was based on REAL Christian grounds. Not the kind of Christianity that blesses war. If Christ were alive now he could not take part. Judge: What would happen if you were attacked? App: That isnt the point, I am fighting for pacifism all over the world. Mr Swales: Have you read the act of Parliament by which you are allowed to stand here? App: Yes. Mr S: Dont be so flippent then. Have you considered that 99 per cent of the Christian faith are willing to take part in war? App: They are not real Christians. The tribunal were shocked at this. App had brought no lettere and no witnesses	In giving the decision the Judge said that this statement was "too fiery" Direct that her name be removed from the register.

N.B. when decision was given App. said "I wont stand by your decision". Gallery applauded

First Woman's Tribunal (TC 6, Box 1/B)

Every Task...(TC 29, Box 3/A)

MASS-OBSERVATION ARCHIVE
Papers from the Mass-Observation Archive
at the University of Sussex
Part 8: Topic Collections - Conscription, Pacifism and War Service
(CONSCIENTIOUS OBJECTION AND PACIFISM; FORCES (MEN);
GAS MASKS; DOGS IN WARTIME)

DETAILED LISTING

REEL 139

CONSCIENTIOUS OBJECTION AND PACIFISM 1939-44

TC6: 3 boxes

There were over 40,000 COs, largely from the middle and lower-middle classes. Many were clerks and local government officers. *"To the conventionally minded some of them looked odd and arty." "...a tendency to be vegetarian, love their mothers, love animals...."* Many were influenced by religious beliefs and belonged to pacifist organisations. Many thought the war was against the principles of Christianity.

TC 6, BOX 1 : LEGAL AND SOCIAL SITUATION OF COs

6/1/A:
"Report on Conscientious Objectors" (July 1940)
Letter: to *New Statesman* with reference to "Report"

6/1/B: Tribunal Hearings for COs
Fulham 18.1.40 (KB)
Bloomsbury 16.1.40 (TB)
Southwark 3.4.40 (PF)
Law Courts 31.8.40 (HP)

REEL 139, TC 6, BOX 1 (continued)

Fulham 14.1.42 (HP)
Fulham 24.2.42 (VT)
First Women's Tribunal: Fulham 25.5.42 (PJ)
Impressions 12.11.40 (JS)
After the Tribunal 26.6.40 (RMF)
Mock Tribunal: Walthamstow 14.3 40 (AFC)
Mock Tribunal: Walthamstow 22.1.40 (AFC)
Opinions on a particular case 23.10.40
Abstract of National Service Act 1939
Sample applications to Tribunal: R Frank, A Tucker, D Spreckley, J Snow, A Hughes, L Ackermann, Jenkins to Ministry of Labour
Appeal Tribunals
 6.12.39 London SW1 (BA)
 2.4.41 'Leonard', London W7
 17.4.41 (DS)
 Leaflets
 "Before the Tribunal' Fellowship of Reconciliation
 Walthamstow and District Advisory Committee for Objectors and Conscripts, Bulletin, March 1940
 Central Board for Concientious Objectors Bulletin, February 1941

6/1/C:
Report on CO Tribunals 2.2.40 (AFC)
Report on Tribunals (6 parts) (JGF)

6/1/D:Press cuttings : CO Tribunals

6/1/E: Employment of COs
Treatment of COs by Birmingham Corporation and establishment of Community Centres 12.11.40 (GOO)
Trade Unions and COs 21.4.40 (JA)
Co-op attitude to COs etc
Jobs of COs 6.40
Christian Pacifist Forestry Units: Letter and Leaflet 25.7.40
Letter from RF 3.12.40
Farm Diary 9.9.40 (RF)
Various Press Reports 28.6.40 (CF)
Various Press Reports
Press cuttings on employment of COs etc

Copy Memo for establishment of pacifist settlement: Lindors Settlement Ltd. 18.3.42

REEL 140

TC 6, BOX 2 : CULTURAL ASPECTS

6/2/A: Various Pacifist Events: Observer Reports
AGM of Peace Pledge Union (PPU) 25.4.42 (PJ)
Adelphi Centre 14.2.42 (MC)
Letter from John Snow 2.10.40
Report on Armistice meeting of Council of Christian Pacifist Groups (CM)
Note on PPU and Quakers (10.40)
"Peace is Possible Now"-Report 3.4.40 (SS)
Observations 19.5.40 (CP)
Letter: PPU Meetings 17.4.40 (CVC)
British Youth Peace Assembly Dance: Report; also PPU meeting 29.5.40
Meeting at Dick Sheppard Centre 10.1.40 (HP)
Various items (KB)
Various items (AFC)
Overheads etc
Debate (report) 28.03.38 Left Bookclub and PPU on Peace
CO Fellowship meeting on prison experiences, Letchworth 24.10.44

6/2/B: Cultural Notes
Notes on "Old Soldiers Never Die" (LE)
Notes on reading and films by John Snow
Note on delivery of *Peace News* (RF)
Summary of *Peace News* 5.1.40 (AFC)
Some circulation figures (JH)
4 analytic tables of CO and Pacifist literature

6/2/C: Pacifism in Great Britain
Pacifism in St. Albans 13.3.40
Pacifist Movement in Great Britain (LO)
The Church and Pacifism
Interview with Rev. Singleton
Interview with Rev. H
Extract from the *Christian Register* April 1940
Extract from *Unity* March 1940
Welsh Nationalists (AFC)

REEL 140, TC 6, BOX 2 (continued)

University Students and the War (Scotland)

6/2/D: Pamphlets, Leaflets etc
National Peace Council
Peace Pledge Union
Fellowship of Reconciliation
Friends Society
Various pamphlets: religious and political
Two photos of people distributing PPU leaflets
Pacifist Service Units booklet

6/2/E: Miscellaneous
Extract from *Manchester Guardian* covering fracas at Royal Ceremony on Armistice Day, November 1938
1 notebook: Tom Harrisson
Handwritten notes: Tom Harrisson
Copies of correspondence of Peter Grant on various issues relating to his conscientious objection
Various correspondence with M-O
Copy *Hansard*, p 678, 11.4.40
Opinion in the RAF
Attitudes in the Forces (Army) to COs 26.11.44 (LE)
Prison experiences: personal reports, August 1944
Various papers, unplaceable

REEL 141

TC 6, BOX 3 : SURVEYS

6/3/A: Pacifist Questionnaire
Sample questions and answers 4.4.40 (BW)
19 answer lists
8 answer lists with additional material, biographical and impressions of subject
1 unplaced sheet signed AFC
3 sheets analytic tables

6/3/B: Pacifism Interview
Fulham: show questions 3.4.40 (HN)

Various: April 1940 (MB)
Attitudes to Churchill, Chamberlain, Russia, Hitler

6/3/C: Pacifism Interview (cont)
Questions 20.8.40 (DH)
Fulham 29.8.40 (CF)
Fulham 28.8.40 (LE)
Fulham 6.4.40 (BA)
Report on COs and Pacifist Activities
"Results of Analysis"-Table and tabulated answers
5 tables
"Pacifist Opinion forming" (BW)

6/3/D: Statistics
Figures from PPU 25.6.40 (RG)
Page of COs in total registration (AFC)
Bulletin of Central Board for Concientious Objectors (January 1940)- giving figures
Press cuttings
Registration figures
3 analytic tables of CO registration under 1939 Act
Press cuttings
6/3/E: Opinion Forming
"Pacifist Opinion Forming" 1 typed page, 24.3.40 (BW)
Memo to TH (pencilled)
Memo to TH (2 sheets typed) on Investigation into opinion forming, 23.3.40 (BW)
Typed memo (4pp) from TH on CO survey 27.3.40

REEL 142

FORCES: MEN IN THE FORCES 1939 - 56

TC 29: 5 boxes

INTRODUCTION
Please note that papers resulting from Mass-Observation's study of women in the Forces have been organised in a separate Topic Collection (TC 32): *Women in Wartime*. This includes attitudes of men towards women in the services.

REEL 142, TC 29, BOX 1 (continued)

Part of the Forces material is composed of reports sent in by voluntary Observers (ie members of Mass-Observation's National Panel) who were in the Forces. As a general rule their regular contributions as Panel members are to be found with the rest of the Panel material (the Directive Replies and Diaries) but special reports such as those on army education and proxy voting have been retained as part of this sequence. The ordinary Directive Replies from Service men are obviously another source of information about life in the Forces and an index of people in the Forces is available in the Archive.

Further material on the Forces may be found elsewhere, specifically in Topic Collection *Work* (TC 27) and Small Collection SM 38 - *World War II Publications*

DW September 1980

TC 29, BOX 1: GENERAL MATERIAL ABOUT THE STUDY; OBSERVATIONS & SOLDIER-CIVILIAN RELATIONS; CONSCRIPTION; RECRUITMENT; THE RAF AND THE AIR WAR; EXHIBITIONS AND FUND RAISING EVENTS

29/1/A: Mass-Observation: Forces Investigations
Internal memoranda about proposals and comments relating to studying men in the Forces
Notes, lists and miscellaneous comments
General correspondence relating to study
Reviews of books about the Forces and articles about the Forces by TH

29/1/B: Observations: the public behaviour of men in the Forces 1939-1940
Overheards, Bolton 1939 (JC)
Observations in London of the behaviour of soldiers, 1939 (AH, HP, BA)
Notes on canteens, London, 1939
Report on members of the RAF and Army in Blackpool, 5.8.40 (AH)
Observation in Bolton, 29.7.40 (BA) and in Stepney, 29.7.40 (NM)
Observations and overheards , London 27.7.40 - 18.9.40 (DH)
Observations and 'follows' in Worcester, 17.7.40 - 21.10.40 (DA)

29/1/C: Attitudes to Conscription 1939
Press cuttings May 1939

Letter from TH re Conscription Survey, 28.4.39
Report of Survey (TH) carried out by EBC, MER, AH, LT, KB, HAC in the East End of London, Norwood, Westminster, Poplar, Streatham and 'in the streets' (434 interviews). Replies to question: "What do you think of conscription?" with analysis sheets

29/1/D: Recruitment 1939
Observations at London recruitment offices made by VMD, KB, JA and BA, November 1939
Notes relating to recruitment
Overheards on conscription gathered in Fulham (LE), 29.7.40
Brief report on an Observer's experience of registration, (LE) 9.11.40
Observation at an Employment Exchange (London?) during the registration of engineers (JS) 19.8.40
Report by JA of his Medical Examination, 8.3.40

29/1/E: Manpower Questionnaire 1941
Replies to questions on the Government's conscription plans including the conscription of women, the conscription of wealth and Government ownership of essential industries (JS, MT, CM) 3.12.41

29/1/F: The Public and soldiers, 1940 - 41
Overheards: comments about soldiers collected by WRL in Uxbridge, DH in Cookham; observations of the behaviour of members of the Forces and public reactions. Reports of conversations with soldiers mostly in London but some reports from Romford, Bolton and Worcester
Civilian-soldier relations: reports, comments and observations
Observations of soldiers on railway stations in London (GD) June 1941
Extract:
"M20B 12/7/40 What is your attitude to soldiers?
'For a long time I felt sorry for them, pitied them, their lives were just being thrown away. But I feel rather different now and I envy them a bit because their minds are made up, they have no doubts as to whether what they are doing is right or whether they are doing the right thing. I still feel very sorry for them, their lives have been messed up especially those about 26 or 27 who have made their names and have got to give it all up without any real reward. The one thing I do not feel is pride in them, because their very existence shows what a hell of a position we're in….' "

29/1/G: Knowledge about the Air Ministry, August 1941
Questionnaire about reactions to Air Marshal Joubert's radio broadcast and

REEL 142, TC 29, BOX 1 (continued)

knowledge about the Air Ministry. Interviews carried out in Bolton, Streatham, Nottinghill Gate and Limehouse

29/1/H: The RAF and the Air War 1940
Envelope of charts identifying German and British aeroplanes published by the *News Chronicle*
Extracts from *The Aeroplane* about aircraft production and preparations for the air war
Notes (TH)

29/1/I: Exhibitions and fund-raising events related to war weapons 1940 - 45
Report from voluntary Observer: War Weapons Week in Chelmsford, 18.4.40 with newspaper cutting
Assorted reports, newspaper cuttings and observations in London areas about War Weapons Week, May 1941
Report on Donnington Tank Week (LE) August 1941
Report on Trafalgar Day Ceremony in London, 21.10.42
Report: Wings for Victory Week in Fulham, 11.3.43
Report: Wings for Victory Week in London, Trafalgar Square, 12.3.43
Report on local activities in Beckenham, 26.6.43
Report on Army Exhibition, London 16.7.43
Report: Army Cadet Exhibition, London, 27.3.44
Report: Salute the Soldier Exhibition, London, 3.4.44
Reports: RAF Exhibition, Dorland House, Regent St, London, 24.4.45
(For printed material gathered at some of the above events, see Box 3)

REEL 143

TC 29, BOX 2: REPORTS FROM INDIVIDUAL MEMBERS OF THE FORCES 1939 - 43

Army
29/2/A: Calder Marshall, A
Reports in the form of letters to TH from Bushfield Barracks, St Cross, Near Winchester written between 1.8.40 and 8.10.40. Includes details of other soldiers and reports on soldiers' reactions to the Blitz
Report from ACM's wife, Ara Calder Marshall in Chiseldon, near Swindon, Wilts, 5.11.40 on the local area and relations between soldiers' wives and

the local residents
Report on morale by ACM including information on training in the Army, 11.6.41

29/2/B: England, L
Notes from former full-time Observer with Mass-Observation, now a Private in the RAOC stationed at Donnington: notes on reactions of fellow soldiers to news items, 25.4.41; letters about possible investigative work inside the Army to be carried out by counsellors

29/2/C: Lee, WR
Reports from Private WR Lee in the Intelligence Corps at Winchester. WRL also a former full-time Observer for Mass-Observation now engaged in top security work. Joins up in November 1940

29/2/D: Novy, H
Detailed and lengthy reports from former full-time Observer now private in the RAMC stationed at Leeds (1.12.40 - 23.2.41), at Catterick, Yorks, (Feb 1941 - April 1941) and at Shotley Bridge, Co Durham (April 1941 onwards) (Further reports on the RAMC and life in Leeds are filed in 66/11/G
Extract:
There are many impressions of the Blitz from a soldier's perspective - and on the impact this had on morale:
"Three factors combine to make morale bad:
1) *Intense worry this week about the home towns that have been bombed.*
2) *Bitter discontent with the way in which applications for leave have been dealt with.*
3) *Complete disinterest about the war as a whole."*

29/2/E: Assorted short reports from other Observers in the Army Royal Air Force

29/2/F: Pepper, C
Reports from A/C 2 Pepper stationed in Torquay, Devon from September 1940 and in Canada from September 1941
CP was a full-time Observer for Mass-Observation before being called up. He later died in action

29/2/G: Papineau, R
Reports and letters to Mass-Observation from LAC Papineau stationed at Blackpool, June 1941

REEL 143, TC 29, BOX 2 (continued)

29/2/H: Picton, R
Account of first medical examination, Ipswich, May 1940
Observations, Alderton, July 1940
Correspondence with TH and reports on RAF life
Selection for Air Crew, Cardington, Beds, August 1940. Stationed at Blackpool (Aug 1940), Torquay (Oct 1940), Newquay (Oct - Dec 1940), Weston-super-Mare (March 1941 - September 1941) where he becomes a Sgt Flying Instructor, Wick (Sept 1941)

29/2/I: Sommerfield, J
Correspondence with TH: stationed at RAF Silloth, Cumberland (1940-41) and at RAF Mellisham, Wilts, July 1941 - Aug 1941
Formerly full-time Observer with Mass-Observation

29/2/J: Assorted material sent in by other Observers in the RAF Royal Navy

29/2/K: Hutchinson, G
Diary, letters to mother and letters to TH with an account of registration at Shepherd's Bush, Jan 1941. Stationed at Skegness (June 1941) and at Torpoint, (June 1941 - Dec 1941)
Additional notes 27.9.43

29/2/L: Miscellaneous reports from Observers in the Navy

REEL 144

TC 29, BOX 3: PRINTED MATERIAL - RECRUITMENT, INFORMATION LEAFLETS, REGULATIONS, ADVERTISING, WAR SAVINGS AND OTHER EPHEMERA 1939 - 45

29/3/A: National Service
General material covering all of the Services including three copies of *National Service* (HMSO 1939), official enlistment forms and other official information for troops

29/3/B: Royal Air Force
Books, leaflets and other official material

29/3/C: Royal Army
Books, leaflets and other official material

29/3/D: Royal Navy
Books, leaflets and other official material

29/3/E: Forces Publications
Official and unofficial Forces magazines with correspondence. Includes *Blighty* (April 1942) and *Jankers* (1941) sent in by Tom Driberg
Typescript: broadcast by Tom Driberg giving advice on producing magazines and papers in the Forces

29/3/F: British Legion
Literature including leaflets about pensions

29/3/G: Miscellaneous ephemera
This folder includes advertising material (eg for uniform suppliers), religious booklets, samples of official stationery, bills, forms, tickets, receipts, labels, ration cards, posters and leaflets etc., material also about Forces entertainments

29/3/H: Overseas Troops
Assorted material about the Services of other nations including the Canadian Army, the Norwegian Air Force and the French Forces

29/3/I: Charitable War Organisations
Leaflets and pamphlets produced by the Red Cross, the Friends Ambulance Unit (including a handwritten report). Relating to Prisoners of War, war relief and mobile canteens

29/3/J: War Savings
Literature from campaigns to encourage war savings: War Weapons Week, Salute the Soldier etc. (see also 29/1/I)

29/3/K: Air Propaganda
Samples of leaflets dropped by the RAF over Germany and German-occupied Europe, 1941

29/3/L: Impact of Blitz on East End
Typed report on effect on soldiers of news of Blitz. 25.9.40

REEL 145

BOX 4: LIFE IN THE FORCES: MORALE, LEISURE, EDUCATION, PAY AND CONDITIONS, PRISONERS OF WAR, THE HOME GUARD AND PROXY VOTING

29/4/A: Life in the RAF, February 1941

Small surveys conducted by Observer D Douglas at RAF Marston, Kent

1. Interviews with 54 Ground Defence men, Fire Staff, Police, Cooks, Drivers and orderlies about their attitudes to being in the RAF, what they miss about civilian life, going to church, their expectations for the postwar period and the possibility of invasion
2. Interviews with 50 RAF men about going out at night, type of entertainment most enjoyed etc

Interviews with 44 airmen about what they missed most from peace time

29/4/B: Public attitudes towards the Army, June 1941

Approx. 200 replies to a 5 point questionnaire about the Army carried out in Kilburn (CF), Hendon (JS), Euston (NN), Croydon (VT) and Oxford (HH)
Tabulations and notes (EL) analysing results of survey

29/4/C: Army Education 1941

Letters from BW to TH about Mass-Observation's study of Army Education (March-April 1941)
Letter from Raymond Gauntlett (1941 Committee) to TH
Copies of *Current Affairs in the Army*: an outline of a new plan (ABCA), *War: News Facts for Fighting Men*, No. 2 and *Current Affairs* No. 1 (1941). All sent to M-O by B Dobree (War Office)
Reports from men in the Forces, April 1941 on educational facilities (includes information on reading habits, special education schemes, course, radio listening habits etc)
Listener Research Report (BBC) 15.4.41

29/4/D: Service Clubs

Brief descriptions of three service clubs in London by GH (Navy), August 1941

29/4/E: Army Pay and Social Welfare
Article in *New Statesman* 10.8.41 about Army pay
Typed manuscript of questions and answers on social services available to members of the Forces and their families (no date)
Special report on pay, 22.9.41 from J Gaston in Luton
Survey conducted by LE in Donnington, November 1941
Extracts from Mass-Observation diaries compiled by YL on army pay and conditions (1941)
Report on pay based on M-O Directive Replies, August 1941 (BW)
Note on army compensation, Stepney (NM)
Army expenses: personal note from LE, May 1941
Report: Soldiers' expenditure in a country unit sent in by HN, RAMC, 22.6.41
Newscuttings and quotations from the press and from *Hansard*, 1941
Indirects on pay, August 1941 collected in Walham Green (MS), Mill Hill and Neasdon (JS & GD)
Notes by JF, 7.8.41

29/4/F: Service Allowances Survey, September 1942
155 replies to a 6 question survey conducted in London areas: Hyde Park (TO), Paddington (LB), Clerkenwell and Holborn (POL), Notting Hill Gate and Marylebone (CM) and Kilburn (CF). Includes attitudes towards increases in Servicemen's pay, dependents' allowances, comparisons with the pay of other nationalities stationed in Britain

29/4/G: Prisoners of War, June 1942
Extracts from letters written by PoWs to their families which were sent to M-O by the Red Cross. All the PoWs in German prison camps 1941 - 42.
Notes by HP

29/4/H: The Home Guard
Reports sent in to M-O by members of the Home Guard 1940 - 44 with leaflets
(Further material on the Home Guard is available in the Topic Collection AIR RAIDS (TC 23))

29/4/I: Proxy Voting in the Forces, July 1944
Reports from members of the M-O panel in the Forces at home and abroad on the availability of information about proxy voting

REEL 146

TC 29, BOX 5: DESERTERS 1947; RECRUITMENT SURVEY 1956

29/5/A: Deserters, March 1947
Opinions about deserters collected informally by BS and HS (no location)

29/5/B: Recruitment Survey 1956
General material about the survey with instructions for interviewers, August 1956, advising personnel that the survey is being commissioned by the Government Social Survey at the request of the Ministry of Defence to assess the effectiveness of recruitment campaigns
Sample questionnaire
Coding sheets

29/5/C: Names and address of interviewees
Lists of the many towns in which the interviews took place
Lists of the names and address of the interviewees

29/5/D:
Tabulations of results with notes

29/5/E:
Computer print out of results

29/5/F:
Miscellaneous papers and press cuts relating to the whole FORCES Topic Collection

REEL 147

GAS MASKS 1939 - 43

TC 55: 2 boxes

TC 55, BOX 1 : GAS MASK CARRYING: GENERAL MATERIAL AND COUNTS 1939 - 40

55/1/A: Gas Tests and Mask Maintenance
Handwritten observations of gas mask testing and fitting of new filters by

ARP wardens; Kensington,Stratford Rd, Queen's Gate, Portobello Rd, 24.5.40 (DH)
Handwritten overheard and impressions of gas mask fitting 24.5.40 (DH)
Typed overheard; gas mask testing 24.5.40 (PF)
Typed observation of ARP wardens preparing for a gas mask testing session 24.5.40 (CF)
Typed observation of fitting sessions for gas mask filters Fulham 24.5.40 (HP)
Handwritten observation; conversation with warden testing gas mask 24.5.40 (CP)
Handwritten table of frequency of gas mask testing by M-O volunteer panel, with comments. Undated
Handwritten report of "Gas Test"; tear gas released in street by ARP for public gas mask practice Esher, Surrey 5.4.41 (JS)
Press cutting *Evening Standard.* Photograph of nurse with baby in gas helmet, Esher gas test 5.4.41
Handwritten report of Esher gas test 5.4.41 (DH)
Handwritten report of Esher gas test 5.4.41 (JS)
Typed report of gas test, East Molesey 5.4.41 (GH)
Handwritten report of Kingston gas test 5.4.41 (JSF)
Typed report of gas tests at East Molesey and Esher, photocopy M-O 8.4.41
Press cutting: photograph and text headed, "Gas test over - No masks" *Daily Mail* 23.6.42
Handwritten special report; "Richmond Gas Week". Index of events and handwritten interviews, observations etc. 18.6.42 (LB)
Press cutting, "To think we've come to this - a baby's gas helmet". Leader from *Manchester Guardian.* Undated
Printed leaflet, "If Hitler uses blister gas", issued by Ministry of Health 16.6.42
Duplicated programme: Richmond Gas Week - 15-20.6.42; list of events and information. Richmond Borough Council
Handwritten overheard, Notting Hill Gate 10.7.40 (DH)
Typed note on gas booby traps, 4.4.41 (VW)
Typed report about dealing with ARP officials issuing gas masks 26.8.39, 2.9.39 (TH)

55/1/B: Gas mask Questionnaire March 1941
Typed 10 point questionnaire about Herbert Morrison's gas mask speech on radio. Possibilities of a gas attack, gas mask habits, and attitudes to gas masks. Observer's impression of replies Hammersmith 29.3.41 (DS)
Typed questionnaire as above; Kilburn 29.3.41

REEL 147, TC 55, BOX 1 (continued)

Typed and handwritten questionnaire replies, approx. 50 replies 29.3.41 (DH, DS)
Handwritten summary of replies 29.3.41 (DH)
Pencilled data tables

55/1/C: Gas mask Questionnaires April and July 1941
Handwritten 8 point questionnaire about government anti-gas leaflet, use of gas masks and how to preserve food from the effects of gas 29.4.41 (DH)
Handwritten questionnaire replies, Letchworth, Notting Hill, Hendon, 100 replies approx. 28.4.41 (DH, CF, JS, GH)
Typed 2 point questionnaire about the day's news and whether interviewee is carrying a gas mask 14.7.41 (HH)
Typed questionnaire replies (12) Oxford 14.7.41 (HH)
Pencilled data tables for 8 point questionnaire

55/1/D: Gas mask Counts 1939
Counts of people carrying (or not carrying) masks in streets and public places. London and provinces, September to December 1939 (Done by full time and volunteer observers)

55/1/E: Gas mask Counts, March to May 1940
Gas mask counts with occasional notes and comments by observers March, April and May 1940

55/1/F: Gas mask Counts, June 1940
Counts as above, with occasional comments June 1940

55/1/G: Gas mask Counts, July to August 1940
Gas mask counts for July and August 1940

55/1/H: Gas mask Counts, September to December 1940
Gas mask counts for September, October, November and December 1940

REEL 148

TC 55, BOX 2: GAS MASK COUNTS 1941 - 43. REPORTS AND CONCLUSIONS

55/2/A: Organising the Gas mask Counts

Typed letter to volunteer observers, asking them to make gas mask counts
Typed instructions to observers," Definition of Gas Mask Doubtfuls" 14.7.42 (DB)
Handwritten notes of suggested methods for gas mask counts 12.3.41 and 20.3.41 (JSF)
Gas mask counts for January, February and March 1941

55/2/B: Gas mask Counts, April and May 1941
Gas mask counts with occasional notes by observers

55/2/C: Gas mask Counts: Draft Reports
Handwritten draft report on Morale and Gas mask Carrying 19.5.41 (JSF). Final report in File L
Handwritten draft report on Gas masks and attitudes to gas. April to May 1941 (JSF). Final report in File L

55/2/D - E: Gas mask Counts: June to September 1941
Gas mask counts for the above period 1941

55/2/F: Gas mask Counts: October to November 1941
Gas mask counts for the above period 1941, some tabulated

55/2/G: Gas mask Counts: December 1941
Gas mask counts for December 1941, some tabulated

55/2/H: Gas mask Counts: January to March 1942
Gas mask counts for the above period 1942, all tabulated

55/2/I: Gas mask Counts: April to May 1942
Counts for the above period with occasional notes by observer's some tabulated

55/2/J: Gas mask Counts: June to August 1942
Gas mask counts with occasional notes and comments by observer's some tabulated, June, July and August 1942

55/2/K: Gas mask Counts: Late 1942 and 1943
Gas mask counts as above for September to December 1942
Brief counts for January to March 1943

55/2/L: Gas mask Counts: Reports and Summaries
Handwritten letter referring to gas mask counts and other M-O business 8.9.39 (CM)

REEL 148, TC 55, BOX 2 (continued)

Typed note on time and place factors in gas mask counts, undated
Typed note on gas mask carrying 26.5.40 M-O
Typed report on "New Gas mask Filter" 25.5.40 M-O
Typed report on "Gas mask Carrying; Regional Differences" 7.6.40 M-O
Typed note on gas mask counts 3.8.40
Typed note on reactions to air raids and their effects on gas mask carrying. 3.8.40
Typed report on "Gas masks", M-O 14.8.40
Handwritten report on gas mask data from the volunteer observers 17.10.40 (JSF)
Typed report on "Attitudes to gas", M-O 31.3.41
Typed report on "Feelings about Poison Gas", 20.4.41 M-O
Typed interim report on Gas mask Carrying 16.5.41
Typed "Further Report on Gas mask carrying", 21.5.41 M-O
Typed report on Gas mask Leaflet 1.6.41 M-O
Printed document: "What to do about Gas", issued by Ministry of Home Security, 1941
Typed report on "Morale and Gas mask Carrying" 11.6.41 M-O
Typed report on "Gas mask Carrying and Newspaper Reading" 12.6.41 M-O
Typed letter to TH from Philip E Vernon, discussing the gas mask survey and other matters relating to morale and wartime psychology. 6.6.41
Photocopy of typed and handwritten report; Quarterly summary of gas mask carrying for April to June 1942 2.7.42 (DB)
Photocopy of typed report; Quarterly summary of gas mask carrying for October to December 1942 1.1.43 (DB)
Coloured graph; Time variations in gas mask carrying 16.5.41

55/2/M
Photocopy of handwritten report; Data from September 1940 directive. Gas masks. 25.5.73 (DW)

REEL 149

DOGS IN WAR TIME 1939-42

TC 79: 1 box only

79/1/A: Dog Organisations in war time 1939-41
Typed interview with man from Canine Defence League on membership, activities, public and government attitudes to dogs in war time, air raid precautions and dogs, London 13.2.41 (DS)
Typed interview with Dog Defence League on same topics as above, London 29.2.40 (JA)
Miscellaneous press cuttings and ephemera:-Typed extracts and press cuttings from newspapers and periodicals on animals in war time, November 1939-January 1940
National Canine Defence League (NCDL) membership form and 2 NCDL pamphlets on war time dog food 22.9.39
"Gas masks for domestic dogs or cats are, in our experience, quite impractical...." (NCDL)
NCDL notice of air raid shelters for people and their dogs, March 1940
NCDL leaflet on air raid precautions for dogs and cats, March 1940
National Air Raid Precautions Animals Committee (NARPAC) appeal for jumble, 8.3.40 (LE)
Advertisement for 'Lustre Lead', dog collar that glows in the dark, March 1940 - *"The Lustre-lead glows with a beautiful fluorescent green colour in the dark - use in the black outs...."*
Advertisement for 'Frank Heaton Protective Enclosure', March 1940
Typed list of pet meat suppliers, March 1940
Pamphlet-'Your Dog and Cat in War Time' produced by Bob Martin, 23.7.41 (VW)

79/1/B: Dog Survey 1941
First pilot survey 11-14.7.41:-Handwritten 6 point QQ on effect of war on dogs i.e. food, air raids, London 11.7.41 (NN)
Handwritten summary of survey, 11.7.41 (NN)
16 handwritten responses to QQ, Euston 11.7.41 (NN)
Handwritten report on methods used for indirects on dogs and general impression of attitudes to dogs, London 11.7.41 (JS)
17 handwritten indirects on dogs, Mill Hill, Hammersmith, Acton, Hendon, Burnt Oak, 11-14.7.41 (JS, VW)

79/1/C: Dog Survey 1941-Second Pilot
Typed QQ with handwritten notes in two sections, one for dog owners and one for non dog owners, 16.7.41
Handwritten criticism of QQ, 16.7.41 (JS)
15 handwritten responses to QQ with investigators reports, 16.7.41-21.7.41 Euston, Willesden (NN, JS)

REEL 149, TC 79, BOX 1 (continued)

Handwritten indirects with dealers and pet shop assistants on availability of pet food and accessories i.e. leads and collars, and how this has been affected by the war, Walham Green, Earls Court Rd, Kensington Church St, Finsbury Park, 30.7.41 (MS, JS, JB)

79/1/D: Dog Survey 1941-Final QQ
15 point QQ with questions for dog owners and non dog owners on keeping dogs in war time 22.7.41
1 carbon copy of QQ 22.7.41
1 handwritten draft of QQ 22.7.41 (NN)
249 typed and handwritten responses to QQ, Hendon, Neasden, Euston, Camden Town, Mill Hill, St Pancras, Willesden, Oxford, Cricklewood, 22.7.41-18.8.41 (NN, JS, DH, HH, PG)
Typed and handwritten analysis, notes and handwritten analysis sheets, 29.7.41-23.8.41 (EL, AH)

79/1/E: Survey of non dog owners-August 1941
Typed report 'Dogs in War Time'-opinions of non dog owners on the keeping of dogs in war time (includes indirects), Cricklewood 26-27.8.41 (PG)
Handwritten summary and indirects with non dog owners on keeping dogs in war time, Euston, Hendon, Neasden, 26-27.8.41 (NN, JS)
Handwritten report 'Opinions of Non Dog-Owners on Dog Keeping in Wartime', 29.8.41 (RF)
Handwritten analysis, 29.8.41 (RF)

79/1/F: Worcester Dog Show-August 1941
Handwritten report on Worcester Dog Show 21.8.41 (DH)
Handwritten note on difficulty in travelling to talk to dog breeders in Worcester 22.8.41 (DH)
Printed card for Worcester Dog Show

79/1/G: Dogs and Bones QQ 1942
56 Handwritten responses to 4 point QQ on whether people give their dogs bones, if not what they do with them (i.e. salvage) and what they think about a ban on dogs being given bones because of the war, Kensington Gardens, Clerkenwell, Hyde Park 11.9.42
There is no copy of the QQ
Handwritten analysis sheets, 11.9.42 (CM, TO)